JOB METHODS

Sessions Outline
and
Reference Material

JOB METHODS

A TRAINING WITHIN INDUSTRY PROGRAM

A plan to help the supervisor produce
greater quantities of quality products in
less time by making the best use of the
manpower, machines, and materials that
are now available.

WAR MANPOWER COMMISSION

Bureau of Training

Training Within Industry Service

1944

Originally published as *Job Methods: Sessions Outline and Reference Material*, released in 1944 by the War Manpower Commission of the Bureau of Training, Washington, District of Columbia.

Enna Products
1602 Carolina St.
Suite B3
Bellingham, WA 98229
Telephone: (360) 306-5369
Fax: (905) 481-0756
E-mail: info@enna.com

Distributed by Productivity Press, an imprint of CRC Press
711 Third Avenue, New York, NY 10017
2 Park Square, Milton Park, Abingdon, Oxon OX14 4RN
www.productivitypress.com

CRC Press is an imprint of the Taylor & Francis Group, an informa business

Cover Design/Illustrations by Khemanand Shiwram
Editor: Collin McLoughlin
Associate Editor: Shawna Gilleland

Library of Congress Control Number: 2009938937

Library of Congress Cataloging-in-Publication Data

United States. Bureau of Training. War Manpower Commission. 1944
        Job Methods: Sessions Outline and Reference Material

        ISBN 978-1-897363-93-5
        1. Training Within Industry   2. Training of employees   3. Organizational change
4. Productivity–Increasing through training

Dedicated to the men and women of The Greatest Generation.

WAR MANPOWER COMMISSION

WASHINGTON, D.C.

September 1943.

To The War Production Trainer:

As you help war production supervisors use this JOB METHODS program, you have a rare opportunity to serve the Nation in this emergency.

You also have a major **obligation** to the Nation, as well as to each supervisor.

The situation is a very practical one. Most of the men with whom you will work have had years of experience. They have latent ideas which, if properly developed, will increase production, reduce lost time, prevent waste of material, and increase the use of machinery and equipment. These men command your respect because of their knowledge.

Your function is to show them how to fully develop their ideas for practical use and present them successfully to their Managements. You have two jobs to do: One is to help the supervisor to acquire skill in the use of this "precision tool" for improving job methods; the other is to improve your own ability in training supervisors how to use it effectively.

You should strive with all the energy and diligence you possess to lead each group in the very best possible way—and to do a still better job with each succeeding group.

To assure a uniformly high standard, you should ALWAYS work from this outline. Never deviate from it. Don't trust to your memory, regardless of how many times you may present the plan. It is not difficult and if you follow instructions you can't fail. Furthermore, you will find it a fascinating job.

Once again, leadership in this Jobs Methods Program presents a **personal opportunity** and an **obligation**.

Sincerely,

C. R. Dooley, Director,

Training Within Industry Service.

SKILL IN IMPROVING JOB METHODS MEETS ONE OF THE

SUPERVISOR'S FIVE NEEDS

1. **Knowledge of the Work**—Materials, machines, tools, processes, operations, products, and how they are made and used.

2. **Knowledge of Responsibilities**—Policies, agreements, rules, regulations, schedules, interdepartmental relationships.

   These two knowledge needs must be met currently and locally by each plant or company.

   Such knowledge must be provided if each supervisor is to know his job and is to have a clear understanding of his authority and responsibilities as a part of management.

3. **Skill in Instructing**—Shortening training time by breaking down each job into units easily learned, making the learner receptive, presenting the instruction, trying out his performance, and following up for results.

4. **Skill in Improving Methods**—Utilizing materials, machines, and manpower more effectively by having supervisors study each operation in order to eliminate, combine, rearrange, and simplify details of the job.

5. **Skill in Leading**—Increasing production by helping supervisors to improve their understanding of individuals, their ability to size up situations, and their ways of working with people.

   These three skills must be acquired individually. Practice and experience in using them enable both new and experienced supervisors to recognize and solve daily problems promptly.

   Training Within Industry Service assists companies in giving their supervisors a start in acquiring these skills through three 10-hour programs: Job Instruction, Job Methods and Job Relations.

   These skills, acquired through this training, must become a part of day-to-day OPERATIONS. In no other way can production be so quickly influenced and manpower conserved.

   Confidence and resourcefulness in how to proceed, not standardized solutions and rules, are developed. These enable supervisors to get good teamwork, to give better service, and to get out more production.

MORE PRODUCTION THROUGH SKILLED SUPERVISION!

SESSIONS OUTLINE

FOR THE

FIVE TWO-HOUR SESSIONS

Paragraphs in quotation marks are to be presented either by using the exact words of the text or expressing the exact meaning in the Trainer's own words. In case of the latter, special care should be taken to convey the exact meaning every time.

Wherever the expression "(some discussion)" appears, there should be brief discussion to make the point clear or to reach agreement with the group.

Words in **bold face** are key words which provide the Trainer with a quick clue to the statement made in the sentence.

BEFORE YOU BEGIN SESSION I

BE SURE YOU HAVE THESE MATERIALS

1	Attendance Record	14	JM Instruction Cards
1	Suggested Introduction	14	Present Method Breakdowns
14	Present Method Layouts	14	Proposed Method Breakdowns
14	Proposed Method Layouts	28	Blank Breakdown Sheets

Demonstration Kit Consisting of:

1	Fixture	1	Stamp Pad
2	Jigs	250	Brass Cards
2	Staplers	250	Copper Cards
		1	"TOP" Stamp

BE AT THE PLANT 30 MINUTES BEFORE SESSION IS DUE TO OPEN

See the Plant Executive. Make certain he is prepared to open the meeting with a suitable introduction. Give him a copy of the SUGGESTED INTRODUCTION if he has not already received one.

BE AT THE MEETING ROOM 15 MINUTES AHEAD OF TIME

Arrange CHAIRS around the conference TABLE. If there is no table, place chairs in the shape of a "U."

Put a FINISHED SHIELD on the table, also ONE COPPER SHEET and ONE BRASS SHEET.

Place TWO CHAIRS, to be used as SUPPLY BOXES, SIX FEET BACK from the table.

Put a supply of COPPER SHEETS on one chair, and of BRASS SHEETS on the other.

Place TWO waste-paper BASKETS to the RIGHT of the table (to serve as SCRAP BINS).

Put one STAPLER, the STAMP PAD, and STAMP on the table.

Place a waste-paper BASKET to the LEFT of the table (to serve as a TOTE BOX).

Put the extra STAPLER, the JIGS and FIXTURE, out of sight of the Group.

Place SAMPLE HAND-OUT SHEETS and INSTRUCTION CARDS on the table.

WORK FROM THE OUTLINE—DON'T TRUST TO MEMORY

OUTLINE FOR SESSION I

*Time
Table*
*Allow
5 min*

1. INTRODUCTION BY THE PLANT EXECUTIVE

References

Suggested introduction.

- Program **name** and **purpose**.

- **Need for Job Methods** in this company.

- Pledge of **cooperation and support**.

- **Schedule** of Sessions II, III, IV and V.

*5 min
to here*

- **Introduction** of the **trainer**.

*Allow
10 min*

2. INTRODUCTION BY THE TRAINER

Establish an informal atmosphere.

See p. 68

- **Write your name** on the blackboard and **state** your **industrial connection**.

- Use **name cards** if possible. Have members put **names** of their departments **on cards**.

- Have **each** member **say** a **word about** his **job**.

- "This is an **informal conference**, similar to Job Instruction Training Sessions. **Ask questions** at any time. **No notes** are necessary."

- Cover the **"five needs" of every supervisor**. (Not over 3 minutes.)

See p. 69

"What is our purpose?"

- "I'm **not** here **to tell** you **how to run** your **jobs or** to **discuss** the **technical** part of your **work**. We **will discuss** one problem common to all of us: **How to improve Job Methods**."

- "This Job Methods **program will help you produce greater quantities** of **quality products** in **less time by making** the **best use** of the **manpower, machines,** and **materials now available**."

- "This **program will not make people work harder**, or in a hurry, as you will see as the program unfolds."

- "We all realize that the **responsibility for production** is **assigned** to us as **supervisors**."

(over)

- **"We must increase production in spite of** acute **shortages** of manpower, machines, and materials."

3

"Why do we need increased production?"

- "This is the **critical year** of the **war**."

- "**Today, thousands** are **risking** their **lives—tomorrow**, thousands **more will face** the same **risk**."

- "**Best quality** fighting **equipment** and **in huge quantities** will help **win** this **war**."

- "**Your** complete **cooperation and support** of this program **will help** to **meet** the **crisis**."

3. JOB METHODS IMPROVEMENT IS NOT A NEW PROBLEM

"Where is the best source of ideas for giving us this necessary increased production now?"

- "It is **the supervisor**, the person **who knows** more about **the jobs** under him than anyone else." (Some discussion.)

- "**Everyone** in this group no doubt **has** some **ideas on how to improve methods**."

- "Perhaps **we have never** fully **developed them all**."

"Job Methods improvement has always been a regular part of every supervisor's job."

- "Most of the **progress** we enjoy **today is** the **result of improvements** in production methods."

- **Cite examples of improvements** on: Automobiles, Radios, Planes. Get **members** to **compare old and new models**.

- "These **results** have been **accomplished by improvements developed** and applied **by** practical **supervisors** like ourselves."

- "**Ordinarily** these improvements are **made slowly**."

- "But, our **fighting forces can't wait**. They **need them today! Time is short!**"

"The purpose of this plan is to make it easier for us to improve our Job Methods."

- "It will provide **a practical plan** to help us."

- "This **plan** has been **tried and proven** in hundreds of war production plants."

- "It was **developed by** practical **industrial men**."

- "**We'll discuss** the **plan** and see **how** it can be **used** on our jobs right now."

4

*Time
Table*

References

- "**During** the *next four* **sessions** each of us **will** have a chance to **use the plan** on jobs in our departments."

- "**A certificate** from the War Manpower Commission will be given to each member who presents an **improvement, attends all five sessions, and pledges to use the plan.**"

*20 min
to here*

- "**I have used** this **plan on my** own **jobs and know** how well **it works**."

*Allow
5 min*

4. DESCRIBE THE USE OF DEMONSTRATION JOB

"**This plan can be best demonstrated by showing how it was applied to an actual job.**"

See p. 69

- "The **job** is **from a war plant—not this plant**."

- "**Observe** this **job in terms of any job** in your own department."

- "The **same** kinds of **improvements** made on this job can be made **on any job which includes one or more of three** basic **types of work.**"

- **Ask members of the group to name the different types of work done in their Departments.**

See p. 70

BLACKBOARD

1.	Material Handling
2.	Machine Work
3.	Hand Work

- "The demonstration job includes **material handling, machine work,** and **hand work. These** are the features to be compared to **your** jobs—**not** this product, **or** this operation."

- "Let's be sure none of us thinks **this plan** doesn't apply to **our work,** just because we don't make this particular product."

Note: Discuss and stress until thoroughly understood.

Describe the job.

- **Product:** Radio Shields. **(Show sample.)**

- **Materials:** Copper and Brass Sheets, 5" x 8" x 1/64" **(Explain** use of **cardboard. Show sample)**

- **Operations:** Inspect, Assemble, Rivet, Stamp, and Pack. **(Explain** use of **stapler** in place of Riveting Machine. **Show stapler, stamp and pad)**

- **Operators:** 4 **men** at 4 **benches.**

- **Work place:** Supply, Scrap, and Tote Boxes.

5. DEMONSTRATE THE PRESENT METHOD

Follow present method layout and present method break-down exactly.

- **Do the job at a good pace.**
  Tell them **what** you are **doing.**

- **Get, inspect,** and **lay out 12 copper** sheets.

- **Get, inspect,** and **lay out 12 brass** sheets.

- **Stack sets** of sheets to the right of Riveter.

- **Rivet** each Set **(Do at least 3.)**

- **Stamp** each Shield. **Pile** Shields on Table.

- **Place** 12 Shields **in tote box.**

- **Carry 75–lb.** tote **box 50 feet to** the **scale.**

- **Weigh and** make out **ticket.**

- **Handler takes** tote **box 100 feet to Packing Dept.**

- **Packer unloads box, puts 200** Shields **in case.**

- **Packer closes, stencils,** and **weighs** case.

- **Empty** tote **boxes returned** by Handler.

HAND OUT PRESENT METHOD LAYOUT

- **Point out flow of material** and bench arrangement.

Discuss the 3 types of work on the demonstration job

- **Material handling**—"Carrying Boxes." (some discussion)

- **Machine work**—"Riveting." (some discussion)

- **Hand work**— "Laying out, Lining up, Stamping." (some discussion)

6. DEMONSTRATE THE PROPOSED METHOD

A better way of doing this job.

*See pgs.
72-74*

- "Let's **look at a better method** of doing this job. It was worked out **by** the **foreman** with the help of an operator—**after they applied** the **Job Methods plan**."

- "**Consider** this **improvement in terms of any job** in your department."

- "First we will see **what** they did, and then develop **how** they did it."

Set up the proposed method and explain the changes.

- "The **sheets** were **delivered onto** the **bench**."

- **Explain and show** Riveting **fixture and guides**.

- **Describe and show jigs** for sheets.

- "**Less experienced operators** were **used** with the new method. More **experienced**, stronger **men** were **upgraded**."

- **Explain slots** for scrap.

- "**Cases** were **placed** at the bench **by the handler**."

Perform the proposed method.

*See pgs.
73-74*

- **Follow proposed method layout and proposed method job breakdown exactly**.

- Place **sheets in jigs**.

- **Pick up sheets and inspect**.

- **Assemble and place in fixture**.

- **Rivet** bottom—then rivet top. **(Do at least 3)**

- **Place** Shields **in front of fixture**.

- **Place** 20 Shields **in case. (Explain count)**

- **Handler** takes Cases **to** the **Packing Department**.

- **Packer closes, weighs**, and **stencils** the Cases.

(over)

7

HAND OUT PROPOSED METHOD LAYOUT

- **Point out flow of material** and Bench Arrangement.

- **Compare with present** method **layout**.

7. RESULTS OF JOB METHODS IMPROVEMENT

Question the Members for Their Estimate of the Improvement in the use of Manpower, Machines, and Material.

- **As to Production?—"Each Operator Produced Three Times as Many Shields Per Day."** (some discussion)

- **As to Machine Use?—"Each Machine Riveted 50 percent More Shields Per Day."** (some discussion)

- **As to Scrap?—"Scrap Material was Reduced from 15 percent to less than 2 percent, due to less handling of sheets."** (some discussion)

- **"Improvements** were made by **making better use of manpower, machines,** and **materials."**

"The operator did not have to work harder or in a hurry on this proposed method."

- "Doing jobs in a **hurry results in bad work."** (some discussion)

- **Act out** a **"speed-up"** of the **present method** to prove the above point. **Actually hurry!**

- "This **would create waste:** the very thing we are trying to eliminate."

- **"Absolutely not one worker should be sped-up in any application of the Job Methods plan!"**

- **"Improved Job Methods give good work**—because production is increased **by eliminating unnecessary parts** of the job—**and making** the **necessary parts easier and safer to do."**

"The principles used in the demonstration apply to all jobs that include material handling, machine work, or hand work."

- "This **demonstration** job is **only a sample job."**

- **"Hundreds** of other **jobs in** the **same plant** were **improved in** the **same way."**

- "Let's **see how** the Job Methods **plan was used by** this **foreman** in making this improvement."

- **"Also** let's see **how** this **plan will help** us make many improvements **on our jobs.**"

- "The details of this **plan** are **printed on** this pocket- sized **instruction card.**"

HAND OUT INSTRUCTION CARDS—1 to each member

NOTE—Clean up the table.

8. PRESENT THE JOB METHODS PLAN

Present the 4-step plan from the instruction card.

- **Read** the **purpose.**

- **Read only** the **4 main steps.**

NOTE—Keep the card in your hand from now on.

- "These 4 **steps** are all that were **used by** the **foreman in** improving this **sample job.**"

- "**Let's apply** the **4 steps to** the **sample job to see how** the **foreman used** this **plan.**"

- "**Also** to find out **how we can apply the plan to our jobs.**"

NOTE—Erase blackboard.

9. STEP 1: Breakdown THE JOB

Read entire STEP 1.

BLACKBOARD

> **STEP 1** - **Breakdown** The Job
>
> List **ALL** Details

"A job breakdown is the starting point for all Job Methods improvements."

- "**Listing all details gives a complete record and accurate picture** of how the **job** is done."

- It **indicates** the **NEED for improvements.**"

- "It **brings out** many **details** about the job **we never realized** were there."

- "A detailed **breakdown gives** us the **facts.**"

- **Cite personal examples** of familiar details difficult to remember: **Buttons—pockets—steps on porches—windows in rooms—etc.**

- "The **more detailed and accurate the breakdown, the more complete the improvements will be.**"

- "**Let's define a detail**—Every single thing that is done, every inspection, every delay."

- **Develop** the first **five details of** the **demonstration** job on the **blackboard** quickly and accurately.

BLACKBOARD

---

1. Walk to box of Copper Sheets
2. Pick up 15 - 20 Copper Sheets
3. Walk to bench
4. Inspect and lay out 12 Sheets
5. Walk to box and replace extra sheets

- Point out **how easily and quickly** these **five details** were **listed**.

- "Here is a **copy** of the **complete breakdown** for this job as **made by the foreman.**"

HAND OUT THE PRESENT METHOD BREAKDOWN

- **Compare** first five details on **breakdown** with those on **blackboard.**

- **Discuss the details.**

- "The **little time** you spend listing details often uncovers **BIG improvements.**"

- **Explain items at top of breakdown sheet.**

- Explain use of **notes column** as **a reminder** of Distances, Tolerances, Waste, Safety, etc.

- Explain the **difference between** the breakdowns for **Job Instruction** and those for **Job Methods.**

- "**In Job Instruction**, only the **important steps** are listed. **A step may include several details.**"

- "Because, when instructing, many **steps** are obvious and need not be listed."

- "**In Job Methods**, on the other hand, **ALL details must be listed.**"

- "Because **nothing** can be **omitted when studying the method** of production."

"A breakdown is an easy, common–sense way to get all the facts about any job method quickly and accurately."

- "**The best place to make a breakdown is on the job; not from memory.**"

- "**Let** the **operators know what** you are doing **and why** you are doing it."

- "Show him the breakdown; let him help you make it; tell him about these meetings; show him the card; do whatever is appropriate; be frank and open."

- "We have seen how **easy** it was **to make** a **breakdown for** the **demonstration** job."

- "**How many** of us **can make a breakdown** of a job in our own department **by listing all details** the way Bill Brown did?"

    Ask for a **show of hands**.

- "**Now** we will **find** out **how** a **job breakdown** is **used in** applying **STEP 2.**"

NOTE—Erase the 5 details ONLY.

10. STEP 2: QUESTION EVERY DETAIL

Read Item 1 of STEP 2.

- "The **success of** any **improvement depends on our** ability to develop a **questioning attitude.**"

- "We must **question everything** that is done; **every single detail** of the job."

- "These **six** very important **questions taught us** practically **all we know.**"

    "**Young people ask questions** to get knowledge. **Many of us stop** questioning things **too soon.**"

- "We must **deliberately question all** the **details** of the job we want to improve."

- "The **answers** to these questions will **give** the **information** we need **to make improvements.**"

- **Ask** Group **members to read** you the **questions**.

```
STEP 2

QUESTION

Why?
What?
Where?
When?
Who?
How?
_____
```

- "These **questions** are **asked in definite order**." (some discussion)

> "Asking **'How' before 'Why' and 'What'** would waste time **if** the **detail was** found **unnecessary**."

- "**ALL questions** should be **asked of each detail before proceeding to** the **next** detail."

- "**Let's examine each** of the six **questions**."

"First—WHY is it necessary?"

- "We **ask** this question **first** for each detail."

- "We want to **distinguish necessary** details **from** those that are **unnecessary or doubtful**."

- "This is a **most important** question."

> "It provides the **information** that **leads to big improvements if** we find **many unnecessary details**."

- "It is often the **hardest** to get **answered** properly."

- "Therefore we **have** a **check question to** make sure we **get sound** and reasonable **answers**."

"Second—WHAT is its purpose?"

- "We want to **find out if** the **detail has** a **useful purpose or adds quality** to the product."

- "**If not**, we will **reconsider** its **necessity**."

- " '**What** is its **purpose**?' is a **check question on 'Why** is it **necessary**?' "

"Beware of taking action on flash ideas for improvements."

- "**As we get** definite **answers** to these questions, **flash ideas** for improvements will come to our minds **rapidly**."

- "**Hold** these **ideas, but note** the **answers on** the Breakdown Sheet."

- "**Don't decide on** anything **yet. Keep** on **questioning. A better** and more complete **idea usually develops**."

- "**If** the **detail** is **necessary—Continue with** the **other** four **questions**."

"Third—WHERE should it be done?"

- "We ask this question **to find the best PLACE** to do each detail."

- "In which **department?** In which **section?** On which **machine, bench,** or **equipment?**"

"Fourth—WHEN should it be done?"

- "We ask this question **to find the best TIME** to do each detail."

- "Should the detail be done **first or last? In what order?** Must it be done **before or after** some **other details?**"

- "**When will** the necessary **men, machines, materials,** equipment, or tools **be available?**"

"Fifth—WHO is best qualified to do it?"

- "We ask this question **to find the best PERSON** to do each detail."

- "**Who** is best for the job **from** the **standpoint of skill? Experience? Physical strength?**"

"Sixth—HOW is 'the best way' to do it?"

- "We **ask** this **of every necessary detail** only **after** we have asked **Where? When? and Who?**"

- "We want **to find** out if there is **a BETTER WAY** to do each detail."

- "**Usually** there is a **better way**, but to find it we **must** first **question** the **'how?'** of the **necessary details**."

Read Item 2 of STEP 2 and comment as follows:

- "These **are** very **important factors** in any job."

- "**Each** item should be **questioned** the **same** as the **details** in the Job Breakdown."

(over)

13

- **Cite** an **example**, if appropriate, as you discuss any of the following:

- "**Materials, machines, equipment,** and **tools** are **often scarce** and hard to get."

- "**A small change in design may make** possible a **big** Job Methods improvement."

- "An **improvement** in the **layout** of the area or the workplace **may save floor or bench space.**"

- "**Poor safety** and **poor housekeeping can** cause **waste** of **lives, time,** and **space.**"

"**Now, let's see how Bill Brown used these questions on the details of his job.**"

- Ask the Group to **follow** the **present method breakdown.**

- "Bill Brown got these answers to his questions."

- "Whenever he got a good 'clue,' he wrote it down in the **notes column.**"

DETAIL No. 1—WALKING.

(Questions)	(Answers)
Why?	**Not necessary if sheets can be**
What?	**moved nearer to bench.**
	(Write in **notes** column: "**No**, if sheets nearer bench.")

DETAIL No. 2—PICK UP COPPER SHEETS

Why?	**Necessary to assemble the shield.**
What?	**Necessary to assemble the shield.**
Where?	**Close to riveter.** (Write: "Close to Riveter")
When?	Any time **before assembly.**
Who?	**Riveting operator.**
How?	Must be a **better way.** (Write: "Better way")

DETAIL No. 3—WALK TO BENCH

Why?	Unnecessary to walk over; Unnecessary to walk back. (Write: "Same as #1")

DETAIL No. 4—INSPECT AND LAYOUT COPPER SHEETS INSPECTION (4a)

Why?	**Necessary to maintain quality.**
What?	**Necessary to maintain quality.**
Where?	At the **riveting bench.**

14

When?	**Just before assembly.**
	(Write: "Just before assembly")
Who?	**Riveting operator.**
How?	Look for a **better way.**
	(Write: "Better way")

LAYOUT (4b)

Why?　**Not necessary, adds no quality** to the product if the sheets are moved close to bench.
(Write: "**No**, if sheets nearer bench")

DETAIL No. 5—WALK TO BOX AND REPLACE EXTRA SHEETS

Why?　If **no** need to **walk** to box to **get** sheets, **no** need to **walk** to **replace**.
(Write: "Same as #1")

DETAIL No. 6—WALK TO BOX OF BRASS SHEETS

Why?　If **no** need to **walk** for **copper** sheets, why walk for **brass** sheets?
(Write: "Same as #1")

DETAIL No. 7—PICK UP BRASS SHEETS

Why?　Same as with Copper sheets.
(Write: "Same as #2")

DETAIL No. 8—WALK TO BENCH

Why?　More walking.
(Write: "Same as #1)

DETAIL No. 9—INSPECT AND LAY OUT

Why?　Same as with Copper sheets.
(Write: "Same as #4")

DETAIL No. 10—WALK TO BOX AND REPLACE EXTRA SHEETS

Why?　More walking to replace sheets.
(Write: "Same as #1")

DETAIL No. 11—WALK TO BENCH

Why?　More walking.
(Write: "Same as #1")

DETAIL No. 12—STACK 12 SETS (CRISS-CROSS)

Why?　Not necessary if layout is not necessary.
(Write: "**No**, if no layout")

(over)

DETAILS No. 13 to No. 20 Inclusive—RIVETING

- "Bill questioned Details 13 to 20 in exactly the same way. He questioned **each** detail **separately**."

- "To conserve time in this meeting, let's just look at the information he noted."

- "On each detail, Bill felt there must be a "better way." (Write: "Better Way" after each)

DETAIL No. 21—STAMPING

Why?   Specification calls for it.
What?   Doubtful—Could find **no** good **reason for** this **detail**. Let's find out why.
(Write: "Find out")

DETAILS No. 22 to No. 30 inclusive—Were questioned by Bill Brown in the same way

- "He **QUESTIONED** the necessity of **CARRYING AND WEIGHING** the tote boxes."

- "And he found that **COUNTING** and **PACKING** could be done **ANYTIME** and **ANYWHERE AFTER** riveting."

- "**While** he was **questioning and getting** definite **answers he did not make any changes**."

*1 hr
15min
to here*

- "**When all details** on the breakdown **have been thoroughly questioned**—then we are ready to **use STEP 3.**"

*Allow
15 min*

11. STEP 3: DEVELOP THE NEW METHOD

Read TITLES of Items 1, 2, 3, 4 of STEP 3.

BLACKBOARD (ADD)

STEP 2	STEP 3
QUESTION	**DEVELOP**
Why?	
What?	
Where?	
When?	
Who?	
How?	

- "**Answers to the questions** asked **in STEP 2 lead to developing** a New Method **in STEP 3.**"

- "**We** can **increase production** only **when details are elim-inated, combined, rearranged**, or **simplified**."

- "**Notice** the **order of** the first four **items**—To `eliminate' after 'simplifying'** would waste time."

Item 1—ELIMINATE unnecessary details.

- "The **answers to Why? and What? lead** us **to eliminate unnecessary** details."

- "**We eliminate** details to **avoid unnecessary use** of Man-power, Machines, and Materials."

BLACKBOARD (ADD)

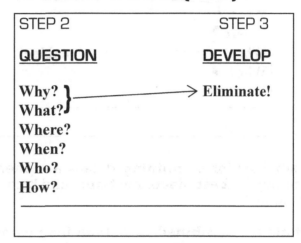

"**Let's see how Bill Brown eliminated unnecessary de-tails.**"

- **Have group** check or **cross off each detail** on the Present Method Breakdown as it is eliminated.

- "From his notes, Bill **decided** that **details No. 1, 3, 5, 6, 8, 10, 11** (Walking) would be **unnecessary if** the **sheets** could be **delivered nearer** the **bench**."

- "Bill found **room on** the **bench** for the supply boxes. He found it was **no extra work** for the **handler**. So **he elimi-nated** all of **these** details."

- "The details **No. 4b, 9b** and **12** (Laying out and Stacking) **added no quality** if sheets were moved to bench—**so he eliminated them**."

- "**Detail No. 21** was found to be **unnecessary**, therefore it was **eliminated**."—**EXPLAIN STAMPING STORY**. *See p. 74*

- "**Details No. 23** and **24** (Carrying and Weighing) served **no** useful **purpose** since Shields were sold by count. So these details were **eliminated**."

(over)

Item 2—Combine details when practical.

- "The **necessary details** should be **combined whenever** it is **practical** and **possible**."

- "The **answers to Where? When?** and **Who? are leads for combining** necessary details."

BLACKBOARD (ADD)

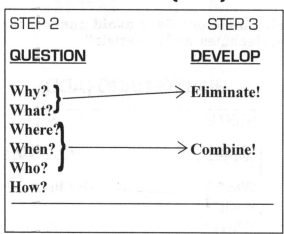

STEP 2	STEP 3
QUESTION	**DEVELOP**
Why? } What?	→ Eliminate!
Where? When? } Who?	→ Combine!
How?	

- "Possibilities for **combining** details are often discovered by finding the **best place, best time** and **best person** to do each detail."

- "**Details** are **combined to reduce inspections** and **handlings** between operations."

"Let's see how Bill Brown combined some of the necessary details on the demonstration job."

- "He had asked of details **Nos. 22, 26, 27—Where? and When?** should the **shields** be **packed and by Whom?**"

- "He **decided** to bring the **cases** to the **bench** and **pack** them there. Therefore the **three** details were **combined**."

Item 3—REARRANGE details for better sequence.

- "If **necessary details can't** be **combined**, they **may be rearranged** for better sequence or order."

- "We **rearrange** details to **reduce handlings and backtracking**."

- "The **answers to Where, When,** and **Who,** also give **leads for rearranging** necessary details.

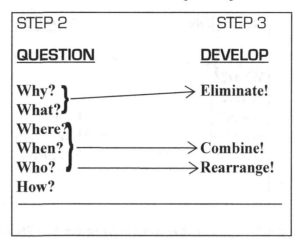

- "**Rearranging** the **order** of details often **saves** unnecessary **moving** of **parts and avoids** unnecessary **picking up** and **putting down** details."

"Let's see how Bill Brown rearranged some of the necessary details on the demonstration job."

- "Because **he** had **changed** the **location of** the **supply boxes**, he had **to rearrange** the details of **picking up** the Copper and Brass **sheets**." (Nos. 2 and 7)

- "Since he **no longer laid out** the **sheets**, he **had to rearrange** the **inspection** details." (Nos. 4a and 9a)

- "It was **not necessary to carry boxes** to the **scale, and** the cases were **packed at** the **bench. So** he **rearranged** the **delivery of cases** to the **Packing** Department." (No. 25)

Item 4—SIMPLIFY all necessary details.

- "We **'simplify' to make** the **necessary details safer and easier** to do."

- "The **answers to How?** give us **leads for simplifying** necessary details."

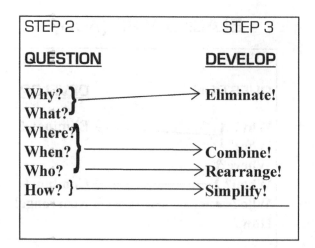

- **Read and explain the principles under Item 4.**

- **Pre-position materials, tools, etc.**
    "To put into the best position for easiest pick up, ahead of time. In racks or holders."
    ... Pen Desk Set.
    ... Tools in rack.

- **Proper work area**
    "Convenient reaching area."
    ... Varies with arm length.

- **Gravity feed hoppers**
    "Using gravity to bring parts to the best place in the work area."
    ... Kitchen match dispenser.
    ... Magazine-feed furnace.

- **Drop delivery chutes**
    "Disposing of a part or piece by dropping it through a chute to a container."
    ... Mail Chute.
    ... Coal Chute.

- **Both hands**
    "Letting the two hands do useful work."
    ... Typewriter... Linotype.
    ... Simultaneous hand assembly.

- **Jigs**
    "*Movable* mechanical holding devices."
    ... Clamp... Guide... Template.

- **Fixtures**
    "*Fixed* mechanical holding devices usually used in connection with a machine."
    ... Tool Rest... Holder.

"Let's see how Bill Brown applied these principles to simplify the details noted—'Better Way.'"

- **Show how** the **proposed methods and work-place** were **developed from** the **card** by Bill Brown and the operator.

See pgs.
78-79

- Start with the **sheets on** the **bench—one riveter**, and **cases** beside the operator.

- **Demonstrate** all **changes** as you describe them.
  (From the card)

- "The sheets were **pre-positioned** in the proper work area."

- "**Jigs** were designed **to hold** the **sheets**."

- "An **angle arm** was added to **make the work easier**."

- "Now **both hands** could do useful work in picking up the sheets."

   "But it was still necessary to **line up** the sheets **by hand—** and to use **one hand for holding**."

- "**A fixture** was designed **to position two riveters**."

   "**Guides** were added **to line up** the **sheets**."

- "Now **both hands** could be used for riveting."

- "**Slots** were cut **in the bench and scrap boxes** were placed **under the bench**."

   So scrap could be discarded by **drop delivery**.

- "**Thickness** of the **fixture** was made so a pile of 20 completed shields was flush with the top."

- "**Cases** for finished shields were **pre-positioned** within **easy reach**."

- "**Gravity feed**—only principle not used."

- "The **principles on** the **card** were **used**—and **only these** principles."

NOTE—The group may offer ideas for further improvements.

- They **may suggest: Foot operated riveters** ... **4 riveters** in one Fixture ... **A bar over** 2 Riveters ... Possibly a woman can do the job.

- **Compliment** the **members for** doing the **right** kind of **thinking**—you **know they** will **apply it to their jobs**.

Review how STEP 2 and STEP 3 are used in order to insure a complete improvement.

- "The answers to **Why? and What?** identify unnecessary **details to be eliminated**."
- "The **answers to Where?, When?, and Who? give leads for combining and rearranging**."

(over)

21

- "The **answers to How? supply leads for** developing `the one **best way**' today **by simplifying**."

Item 5—Work out your idea with others.

- "We can often get **VALUABLE IDEAS** from the '**BOSS**.' "

    "He is the one who knows what changes will take place and where more production is necessary."

    "He can give us practical leads."

- "We can get **help from fellow supervisors**." (some discussion)

- "Our **operators** can **help** us. Working out an idea **with** an **operator** is **especially** important." (some discussion)

- "Remember how **Bill Brown** 'worked with' one of his operators."

    "**Operators** have **good ideas** too; often just as many as **we** have—**sometimes more**!"

    "**Don't** work out an idea and **spring** it on an operator. **None** of **us** would like that. Neither would the operator."

    "When he **helps** work out an idea he gets **real satisfaction**."

- "An **interested** and **satisfied worker** is just as **important** as the **idea** itself."

- "**Usually everyone** is **glad to help if we ask him**."

Item 6—Write up your proposed new method.

- "**Many ideas 'die' before** they are **put into effect or** are **written down**."

- "**Write up exactly what** your **new method will do and how** it can be **done**."

- "**A written proposal is a** complete **summary of** your proposed **improvement**."

- "We **will discuss how to write** up a **proposal** in detail, **during Session II**."

- "**After we have** made a **job breakdown—questioned** every detail—**and developed** the New Method—we are prepared to **put it to work**."

12. STEP 4: APPLY THE NEW METHOD

Read entire STEP 4.

BLACKBOARD (ADD)

STEP 4—APPLY The New Method

- **"Improvements are of no value unless put to work."**

- "Using **STEP 4 insures** the **success** of improvements."

- **"Lack of STEP 4**, in the past, **has prevented many** good **improvements** from **being put to work."**

Item 1—SELL your proposal to the BOSS.

BLACKBOARD (ADD)

STEP 4—APPLY The New Method

Sell—

- "To **get** his **approval for** a **trial**."

- **"Give** him a **short, complete story—facts only—**in your written proposal."

- **"Use breakdown sheets, samples, sketches."**

- **"Put it up to the boss at the appropriate time—**Watch your timing!"

HAND OUT PROPOSED METHOD BREAKDOWN

- **Compare with present method breakdown. Show how** they can be **used as** a **selling story.**

- **"Also use written proposals to explain what** this improvement will do **and how it can be done!"**

- **"List production increases and better uses** of Manpower, Machines, Material, Space, Equipment—**also quality and safety** improvements."

Item 2—SELL the new method to the OPERATORS.

(over)

- "So it will **get a fair test**."

- "**Perhaps** only **one** helped develop it, **but several** will have to **use it**."

- "**Instruct** Operators in new methods **carefully. Use** the **Job Instruction plan**."

- "**Get** the **operators' cooperation and ideas** on all improvements." (some discussion)

Item 3—Get FINAL APPROVAL of all concerned on SAFETY, QUALITY, QUANTITY, COST.

BLACKBOARD (ADD)

> **STEP 4—APPLY** The New Method
>
> Sell—Approvals—

- "Getting **approvals will prevent trouble**."

- "**Get approval of** immediate **supervisor on all factors**."

- "Where necessary, get approval for:"

  - "**Safety**—Safety Engineers and Operators."
  - "**Quality**—Inspectors and Laboratory."
  - "**Quantity**—Production and Planning Depts."
  - "**Cost**—Cost Department."

- "**Follow** regular **organization lines**."

Item 4—PUT the new method TO WORK—use it until a better WAY is developed.

BLACKBOARD (ADD)

> **STEP 4—APPLY** The New Method
>
> Sell—Approvals—Use—

- "**Avoid waiting**, get **action** as **quickly** as possible. **Waiting 'kills'** more **ideas** than lack of brains." (some discussion)

- "**Right now** is the time when **we need every** practical **improvement working** for us."
- "**Check** to be sure **the operators** don't slip back to the old, more familiar method."

- "Remember there **will always be a better way. Keep searching** for further **improvements**."

Item 5—Give CREDIT where credit is due.

BLACKBOARD (ADD)

> **STEP 4—APPLY** The New Method
>
> Sell—Approvals—Use—Credit

- **"One stolen idea will stop all others."**

  "Stopping ideas is sabotage."

- "We want to **be sure we give proper credit and show** sincere **appreciation**."

  "**Ask** the **boss to say a word of appreciation** to the person who made or helped with the improvement."

- The **more credit** we give the more ideas we get."

13. SELL THE USE OF THE JOB METHODS PLAN

Review the 4-step plan.

- **Read each step and the main items** under each.

- "These 4 **steps** were all the **foreman used** to make the improvement **on** the **demonstration job**."

- "These **principles** are **all we need to make** thousands of valuable **improvements**."

- Stress **importance of LEARNING** Instruction **CARD**.

"Would more improvements right now—today—help you with your present production problems?" (some discussion)

- Use the following 5 paragraphs if more "selling" is necessary:

  "**One** improvement **each week** would **make** any Supervisor's **job easier**, reduce **'bottle-necks' and cut down** the number of **'trouble'** jobs."

  "One **improvement today** is worth **ten times as much now** as it would be next year."

"**We can't afford to be `TOO BUSY'** to find time to continually search for improvements."

"**Our** fighting **forces need greater quantities** of **quality products** in **less time to win** this **war.**"

"**Improvements must be made now!**"

"**Will this Job Methods plan make it easier for you to develop and apply improvements?**" (some discussion)

- **If any say "no," point out** that the **plan will help on any** production **job** that includes Material Handling, Machine Work, or Hand Work.

- **To breakdown**, "Our work is different" **attitude, point out** that these **principles** have been **applied by others** to:

  Mass Production and Job Shops.

  Process, Assembly, Machine-tool, and Foundry Work.

  Airplanes, Tanks, Guns, Ships, Munitions, Chemical and Lumber Manufacturing.

- **Get all to agree** that, "**It can be done.**"

14. ASSIGN IMPROVEMENT DEMONSTRATIONS FOR SESSION II

"**This is the whole story—Let's put it to work.**"

- "**Everyone will make** Job Methods **improvements.**"

- "**Pick out a short job in your department** on which you need Greater Quantities of Quality Products in Less Time. Perhaps, **one** that's **giving** you **trouble.**"

- "**Don't try to find** one that might show **startling improvement.**"

- "Take **any job**—perhaps the **first** one that you think of—or the **first** one you **see** as you walk through the department."

- "Make a Job **BREAKDOWN of the present method.**"

- "**QUESTION every detail** on the breakdown."

- "**DEVELOP** the new method."

  "Make a **Proposed Method Job Breakdown.**"

  "If you **don't find** an **improvement on** the **first job, tackle another** one."

- "Get ready to **tell us how you APPLIED or will APPLY** the **new method**."

- "Bring **breakdowns** and **samples, sketches, material, equipment,** and **tools to show both** the **present** and **proposed methods** to the Group."

- "About **20 minutes for both methods**."

- Ask **members to name** the **job** they will "tackle" for improvement.

- **"DO NOT BRING in any SECRET PRODUCTS or processes. Check this with your boss."**

Assign 3 improvement demonstrations for Session II.

- **Get 3 volunteers** for Session II.

- "**Any short job** in your own **department**."

- "**All improvements must be NEW IDEAS**—no ancient history!"

- **Be sure they understand exactly what to do** for Session II.

- **Have them tell you** what they are going to do.

HAND OUT BLANK BREAKDOWN SHEETS

2 to **each** member—1 for **present**, 1 for **proposed**.

15. RESISTANCE AND RESENTMENT—AND CLOSING

"Two human failings have stopped many improvements from being put to work."

- **"The first of these is RESISTANCE to new ideas."**

- "Don't be surprised if someone with whom you are checking over an idea tells you, 'The Present Method has been successful for twenty years—**why change it?**' That is a **natural** reaction."

- "**Be careful of** the natural **resistance everyone** seems to **have** toward new improvements."

- "We **all** tend to **defend past practice, precedent, tradition, custom, habit**—and to argue against any new ideas."

- **Cite** some **examples** of resistance to such things as: Balloon Tires, Hydraulic Brakes, Clipper Planes.

27

- "**Don't let resistance interfere** with improvements."

- "The **principles of the Job Methods plan** are **not new.** They were **developed thirty years ago.**"

- "Job Methods is a **streamlined and simplified** version of tried and proved **principles.**"

"The second failing is RESENTMENT of criticism."

- "Perhaps **someone may interpret** our **search for a better method as personal criticism.**"

- "It is **up to us to explain our purpose, which is** a constructive search for a better way **to get out the production needed for** the **war effort.**"

- "**Let's not be afraid to** bring in improvements that may **infer criticism of ourselves,** i.e. `Why didn't you think of that one before?'"

- "**Our discussion of each** job **improvement will be** only **constructive, not personal criticism.**"

- "Let's **be sure** that **fear of criticism doesn't stop** any of our **ideas** for improvements."

Close promptly with these remarks.

- "**Remember the job we** all **have to do** in this War of Production."

- "Keep in mind that **improving Job Methods is** part of **our fighting assignment.**"

- Stress how **Job Methods improvements will help** in our drive to **produce greater quantities** of **quality products** in **less time.**

- "**Learn** the **instruction card** before Session II."

- "**Remember** your **assignments** for Session II."

- "Bring in **breakdowns, sketches, materials, etc.**—for actual demonstrations."

Session II will be held on:

_____ from _____ to _____
   (Day)   (Hour)   (Hour)

- **Collect name cards** for use at other Sessions.
   Record Attendance.

BEFORE YOU BEGIN SESSION II
BE SURE YOU HAVE THESE MATERIALS

Extra JM Instruction Cards   14 Proposal Sheets
Extra Blank Breakdown Sheets   3   Proposal Reports
14 Example Proposals   Attendance Record

BE AT THE MEETING ROOM 15 MINUTES BEFORE SESSION IS DUE TO OPEN

Arrange chairs. Look after ventilation, blackboard, chalk, erasers, etc.

REMEMBER

In Session II the emphasis is on STEP 1: Breakdown the job.

WORK FROM THE OUTLINE—DON'T TRUST TO MEMORY

If you are invited to visit operation in the Plant, BE ABSOLUTELY SURE YOU DON'T YIELD TO THE TEMPTATION OF GIVING AN "EXPERTS" OPINION AS TO IMPROVEMENT OF ANY OPERATION YOU OBSERVE.

OUTLINE FOR SESSION II

1. OPENING THE SESSION

Opening remarks.

- **Keep** the **meeting informal**.
  Hand out **name cards**.

- **Express appreciation of the group's interest** in improvement of Job Methods as indicated by their coming promptly.

- "We **have seen** how the **4-step** Job Methods **Plan** was **applied to** a **sample job**."

5 min
to here

- "We will now see how these principles can be applied to our own jobs."

2. REVIEW SESSION I

Allow
10 min

Review purpose and 4 steps of the Job Methods Plan.

- **Emphasize** the **purpose**.

- **Have** the **group** give you the **4 steps and** the **main items** under each.

BLACKBOARD

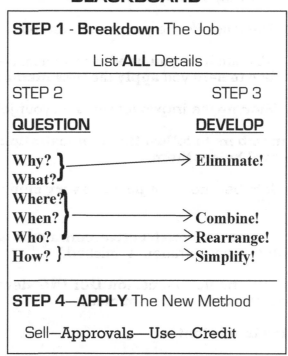

```
STEP 1 - Breakdown The Job

          List ALL Details
_____

STEP 2                      STEP 3

QUESTION                    DEVELOP

Why?  ⎫
What? ⎭ ──────────→ Eliminate!
Where?⎫
When? ⎬ ──────────→ Combine!
Who?  ⎭ ──────────→ Rearrange!
How?  } ──────────→ Simplify!
_____

STEP 4—APPLY The New Method

   Sell—Approvals—Use—Credit
```

- **Review** the **use of each step and each item** as you put them on the blackboard.

(over)

31

- Stress the **relation of STEP 2** to **STEP 3.**

3. PRACTICE DEMONSTRATIONS—TWO JOBS

*Allow
1 hr
20 min*

"The purpose of each demonstration is to learn by doing."

- **"When** we're **convinced** the **plan** can be **practically applied, we can make many improvements."**

- "We are **interested in both** the **improvements and** the **application of** the **4-step plan."**

"To get maximum benefit and to make the demonstrations clear to everyone each member will follow this procedure."

- **Brief the following 8 points on the blackboard:**   *See p. 75*

    1. "**Describe** briefly the **job** you have 'tackled' and explain samples and sketches you will use."

    2. "Demonstrate the **present method."**

    3. "**Show present** method **breakdown and read details."**

    4. "Explain **what information** and leads you **obtained from** the **answers to** the **questions in STEP 2."**

    5. "Explain **how** this **information helped** you to **eliminate, combine, rearrange, and simplify** details **while developing** the **new method in STEP 3."**

    6. "Demonstrate the **proposed method."**

    7. "Explain **how you used**, or will use, the items under **STEP 4 to help** you **apply** the **new method."**

    8. "**Sum up** the **improvements** on your job."

Ask group members to follow the demonstration with the Job Methods instruction card before them.

- "**Check** to be sure **each part of every step** has been considered."

- "Make **notes for constructive comments and** for **questions** *after* demonstration is finished."

- "There will be **no discussion DURING demonstration—** only questions on points **not clear."**

Call on the first volunteer

- **Ask** the volunteer: "Is this **improvement new?** Have you made a **present and** a **proposed breakdown?"**

- If **either** answer is **"No," call** on the **second volunteer.**

- **Have** the **volunteer follow** the **demonstration procedure** outlined above.

How to comment on each demonstration.

- **Compliment** the **volunteer on** the **good points** that show proper application of the Job Methods Plan.

- Ask **members** if there are **questions about** the **demonstration** they want to ask or further improvements they want to suggest.

- **Discuss** the **application of each part** of the 4 steps and exactly how they helped the supervisor make his improvement.

- **Stress:**—"Was it **worked out with** the **operator(s)?**"—"**How was credit given** (or planned)?"

Be sure you don't take the attitude of an "EXPERT." You should ONLY LEAD THE DISCUSSION.

- On **questions involving company policy**, the **supervisor** should be **referred to his own management**.

- **Sum up** the **results** of the **improvements** in terms of increased production and machine use, savings in materials, better quality, safety, and housekeeping, etc. (use blackboard)

- **Record each improvement on the Attendance Record** and the **Proposal Report**.

Stress the use of STEP 1 on each demonstration.

- The **correct** way to make a **breakdown** should be **clearly and completely explained before proceeding** to the next demonstration.

- Show **how** easily a **breakdown** can **PROPERLY** be **made** by **using** the **volunteer's job**.

- **Write** out **on** the **blackboard** entire **present breakdown** (or a substantial part).

- Repeat the **definition of** a **detail:** "Every single thing that is done, every Inspection, every Delay."

- Stress **advantage** of plenty **of notes**.

- Emphasize the **value of** the **breakdown**.

- "We **cannot investigate** all **details properly before listing** them **carefully**."

- "We **must have all** the **facts**."

(over)

33

- "The **success** of the improvement **depends on information obtained from** questioning a **complete breakdown**."

Call on the second volunteer (if time permits).

- Use **same procedure** as with **first volunteer**.

- Be sure to **sum up carefully all improvements** in the demonstration (use blackboard).

- **Record the improvement on** the **Attendance Record and** the **Proposal Report**.

- **Continue to stress** importance of the **breakdown**.

- **List** all **details on** the **board to** further **emphasize** the **importance of** the **breakdown**.

- Use both **present and proposed** methods if necessary.

- Prove that a **breakdown** of the Present Method **listing all details and facts makes it easy to "question"** thoroughly **and** to "**develop**" completely.

4. EXPLAIN USE OF THE PROPOSAL SHEET

Explain importance of writing up proposed new method.

- "Too **many** proposed **improvements 'die' before** they are **put into practice or** put down **on paper**."

- "The **write-up is** a good **device for SELLING** the improvement **to the boss**."

- "It is very **useful in getting final approval** on Safety, Quality, Quantity, Cost, etc."

- "Practical **improvements** can be **passed on and used by others** in the Plant."

How to write up a proposal

- **HAND OUT SAMPLE PROPOSAL**

- **Read** the **proposal and discuss** it in detail.

- "It is **important to list** the **improved uses** of Manpower, Machines, and Material **at the beginning of** the **proposal**."

- "Improvements in **quality, design, safety, housekeeping**, etc., should **also** be included."

- "We must tell **exactly how** the **improvement** can be **made and what** will be **accomplished**."

- Stress the **importance of heading, signature, samples, sketches**, and **job breakdown** sheets.

- "The names of **those who** should **receive credit** should **also** be **shown**."

- **Explain how** the **check list** of **questions on** the back of **proposal** sheet should be **used**.

  "The **questions** will help us **check** the **completeness** of our improvement."

  "They may **give** us some **new ideas**."

  "At least, they will **stimulate** our **thinking** on improving the job."

"Each member will write up a proposal."

- "It should be written-up similar to the **sample**."

HAND OUT PROPOSAL SHEETS

- "Those **who put on** their **demonstrations** are now ready to **write up proposals** in final form."

- "These **members** will **read** their **proposals** to the Group **during Session III**."

- "**Others** will **wait until after** the **demonstrations** to write up and present their proposals."

5. ASSIGN DEMONSTRATIONS FOR SESSION III

Ask for 4 volunteers for Session III demonstrations.

- "Any **short job** in your department. **Not** a **secret** product or process."

- "Tackle the **first job you come to** when you walk into your department."

- "**All demonstrations** must be made by applying **this Job Methods plan**."

- "We **don't want** a review of **improvements** that have been **already** put **in effect**."

- "Each Volunteer will **make** a **job breakdown** of the job he has selected—**question** every detail—**develop** a New Method—**and** work out a **plan for applying** the New Method."

- "Also make a **breakdown** of the **new method**."

- "If you **can't improve** the **first** job you tackle; **breakdown, question**, and **develop another** one."

- Ask **each** Volunteer to **name** the **job** on which he will apply the 4-Step Plan.

- **Have volunteers tell** you **what they are going to do** to follow the 4-Step Plan.

- **Check** with the others in the **group to be sure all** are **working on** a **job and** all are **using** the **4-step plan.**

- "Demonstrations are scheduled for **20 minutes for both present and proposed** methods."

- Invite **any who want help** to **stay** after Session.

6. REVIEW AND CLOSING

Review.

- Stress the value of **learning** the **purpose**, the **4 steps and** the **items** under each step.

- **Review** the use of the **proposal sheet and** the **check list** of **questions**.

Closing the session.

- **Sell** the idea that **"learning by doing"** is the **only way to gain confidence**.

- "Job Methods **improvement is** a regular **part of** the supervisor's **daily job.**"

- Point out the **personal advantage to** supervisors who **make good improvements regularly**.

- Stress the value of having their **proposals carefully worked out** with everybody concerned **before turning them in** for final approval.

- **Close promptly** with the reminder that Session III will be held on

_____ from _____ to _____
   (Day)   (Hour)   (Hour)

- Collect **name cards.** Record attendance.

BEFORE YOU BEGIN SESSION III

BE SURE YOU HAVE THESE MATERIALS

Extra JM Instruction Cards
Extra Blank Breakdown Sheets
Attendance Record

Extra Proposal Sheets
Proposal Reports

BE AT THE MEETING ROOM 15 MINUTES BEFORE SESSION IS DUE TO OPEN

Arrange chairs. Look after ventilation, blackboard, chalk, erasers, etc.

REMEMBER

The emphasis in Session III is on STEP 2: Question every detail.

WORK FROM THE OUTLINE—DON'T TRUST TO MEMORY

OUTLINE FOR SESSION III

1. OPENING THE SESSION

*Allow
5 min*

Opening remarks.

- Hand out **name cards**.

- **Express** your **appreciation of** the **interest** shown by the group at the last Session.

*5 min
to here*

- **Compliment those who presented** constructive **improvements** during Session II.

*Allow
5 min*

2. REVIEW SESSIONS I AND II

Review the purpose, the 4 steps, and the proposal sheet.

- **Stress** the importance of **using** the Job Methods **plan to make** the **best use of all** the Manpower, Materials, and Machines now **available**.

- **Have** the **group** tell you the **4 steps**. Have them **put** their **cards in** their **pockets** during the review.

- **Review** the use of **EACH STEP** as you put it on the board.

BLACKBOARD

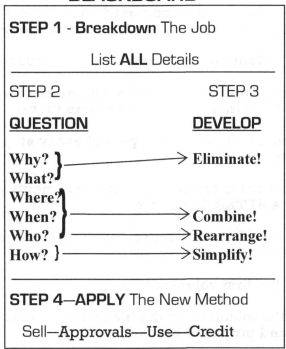

STEP 1 - **Breakdown** The Job

List **ALL** Details

STEP 2	STEP 3
QUESTION	**DEVELOP**

Why? ⎫
What? ⎭ ⟶ **Eliminate!**

Where? ⎫
When? ⎬ ⟶ **Combine!**
Who? ⎭ ⟶ **Rearrange!**
How? ⎫ ⟶ **Simplify!**

STEP 4—**APPLY** The New Method

Sell—Approvals—Use—Credit

*10 min
to here
(over)*

- **Review use** and importance **of proposal sheet.**

Time
Table
Allow
1 hr
40 min

References

3. PRACTICE DEMONSTRATIONS—FOUR JOBS

Stress the value of demonstrations.

- "**Learning by doing gives** us **confidence.**"

- "We see the **practical application** of these principles **to our jobs.**"

- "**Every one** of us **has** the same **opportunity** to **show his ability** in making improvements."

Ask each volunteer to follow this procedure.

- **Brief the following 8 points on the blackboard:**

    1. "**Describe** briefly the **job** you have 'tackled' and explain samples and sketches you will use."

    2. "Demonstrate the **present method.**"

    3. "**Show present** method **breakdown and read details.**"

    4. "Explain **what information** and leads you **obtained from** the **answers to** the **questions in STEP 2.**"

    5. "Explain **how** this **information helped** you to **eliminate, combine, rearrange, and simplify** details **while developing** the **new method in STEP 3.**"

    6. "Demonstrate the **proposed method.**"

    7. "Explain **how you used**, or will use, the items under **STEP 4 to help** you **apply** the **new method.**"

    8. "**Sum up** the **improvements** on your job."

Ask group members to follow the demonstration with the Job Methods instruction card before them.

- "**Check** to be sure **each part of every step** has been considered."

- "Make **notes for constructive comments and questions to use AFTER** demonstration is finished."

- "There will be **no discussion** during **demonstration**—only questions on points not clear."

Call on the first volunteer

- **Ask** the volunteer: "Is this **idea new**? Have you made a **present and proposed breakdown?**"

    If either answer is **"No," call** on the **next volunteer.**

- **Have** the **volunteer follow** the **demonstration procedure** outlined above.

How to comment on each demonstration.

- **Compliment** the **volunteer on** the **good point**s that show application of the Job Methods plan.

- Ask **members** if there are **questions about** the **demonstration** they want to ask or further improvements they want to suggest.

- **Discuss** the **application of each part of** the **4 steps** and exactly how they helped the supervisor make his improvement.

- Stress: "Was it **worked out with** the **operator(s)?**"—"**How was credit given** (or planned)?"

- **Be sure you do not assume the attitude of an "expert." You should ONLY LEAD the discussion.**

- On **questions involving company policy**, the **supervisor** should be **referred to** the **management**.

- **Sum up** the **results of** the **improvements** in terms of increased production and machine use—savings in materials—better quality, safety, and housekeeping—etc. (use blackboard)

- **Record each improvement on** the **Attendance Record and** on the **Proposal Report**.

Stress the use of STEP 2 during this practice period.

- **Stress** the **importance of** a **questioning attitude** throughout this Session.

- Get the group to ask **Why? What? Where? When? Who? How? Questions** during the discussion after each demonstration.

- Review the **relation** of **Step 2** to **Step 3**.

- Stress the **importance** of **asking** each **bracket** of **questions** for **each** detail.

- Emphasize the **need** for **holding back "flash ideas"** and noting them on the breakdown sheets.

- "The **best improvements** are **developed** only after **careful** and **complete questioning**."

- Explain **why** it is **essential to complete STEP 2 before starting STEP 3**.

- Stress the **importance of questioning** all **factors in Item 2** of STEP 2 and **how these** may **affect** the **details** of the job.

(over)

41

Demonstrations No. 2, No. 3, No. 4 (same as No. 1).

- **Sum up** the **improvements** on each job. (use blackboard)

- **Record each improvement on Attendance Record and on Proposal Report**.

"The four members who put on demonstrations will write up their proposals and read them at Session IV."

4. PROPOSALS ON SESSION II DEMONSTRATIONS

Ask members who put on demonstrations during Session II to read their written proposals.

- Ask for **comments and suggestions**.

- **Recommend** that the **proposals, breakdown sheets**, sketches, and samples **be submitted at once for approval and action**.

- **Record results of improvements on Proposal Report**.

5. ASSIGN DEMONSTRATIONS FOR SESSION IV
—AND CLOSE

Ask for volunteers for Session IV demonstrations.

- "Any **short job. Not a secret** product or process."

- **"Must be NEW improvements."**

- **"Follow** the **4-step plan."**

- "Make a **breakdown** of the **proposed method."**

- **Check** the **jobs** with volunteers.

- Invite **any who want help** to **stay** after Session.

Closing the session.

- Point out the high points of each demonstration and **compliment** the **group on** their **progress**.

- Remind the group that **similar improvements will** go far to **help win the war**.

- **Emphasize** the **urgent need for every improvement**.

- **Stress** the value of **taking time to** develop New Methods that **save time, machines and material**.

42

Time
Table

- **Close promptly** with a reminder about Session IV
  on

_____ from _____ to _____
(Day)   (Hour)   (Hour)

End of
2 hr

- Collect **name cards**. Record attendance.

BEFORE YOU BEGIN SESSION IV

BE SURE YOU HAVE THESE MATERIALS

Extra JM Instruction Cards
Extra Blank Breakdown Sheets
Attendance Record

Extra Proposal Sheets
Proposal Reports

BE AT THE MEETING ROOM 15 MINUTES BEFORE SESSION IS DUE TO OPEN

Make an appointment with the Plant Representative to see him on the day Session V will be held, 45 minutes before it opens. The object is to review with him the Methods Improvements presented at Session II, III, and IV which you have listed on your PROPOSAL REPORT.

Between the close of Session IV and the time of your appointment, prepare the PROPOSAL REPORT you will discuss with the Plant Representative.

In the Meeting Room arrange chairs, look after ventilation, blackboard, chalk, erasers, etc.

REMEMBER

The emphasis in Session IV is on STEP 3: Develop the new method with others.

WORK FROM THE OUTLINE—DON'T TRUST TO MEMORY

OUTLINE FOR SESSION IV

References

1. OPENING THE SESSION

Opening remarks.

- Hand out **name cards**.

- **Express** your **appreciation of** the **interest and enthusiasm** shown by the group.

- **Compliment those who presented** constructive **improvements** at Session III.

- **Stress** the **need for** developing **improvements** and for getting action so they will be put into effect.

- **Ask if** the **improvements** proposed during Sessions II and III **have been put into effect**.

5 min
to here

NOTE—This will give you something concrete to talk over with the plant representative.

Allow
5 min

2. REVIEW PREVIOUS SESSIONS

Review purpose and 4 steps of the Job Methods Plan.

- Ask a **member to state** the **purpose without** looking at the **instruction card**.

- Ask the **group** to **develop** the **4 steps without** using the **card**.

BLACKBOARD

STEP 1 - **Breakdown** the Job
STEP 2 - **QUESTION** every Detail
STEP 3 - **DEVELOP** the New Method
STEP 4 - **APPLY** the New Method

10 min
to here

- **Point out** some outstanding **applications of** the **4 steps in** Session III **demonstrations**.

Allow
1 hr
35 min

3. PRACTICE DEMONSTRATIONS FOUR JOBS

Point out the advantage to all members of applying the Job Methods principles to all jobs.

(over)

- "The **demonstrations** at Sessions II and III **illustrated** the **importance of learning by doing**."

Ask each volunteer to follow this procedure.

- **Brief the following 8 points on the blackboard:**

    1. "**Describe** briefly the **job** you have 'tackled' and explain samples and sketches you will use."

    2. "Demonstrate the **present method**."

    3. "**Show present** method **breakdown and read details**."

    4. "Explain **what information** and leads you **obtained from** the **answers to** the **questions in STEP 2**."

    5. "Explain **how** this **information helped** you to **eliminate, combine, rearrange, and simplify** details **while developing** the **new method** in **STEP 3**."

    6. "Demonstrate the **proposed method**."

    7. "Explain **how you used**, or will use, the items under **STEP 4 to help** you **apply** the **new method**."

    8. "**Sum up** the **improvements** on your job."

Ask group members to follow the demonstration with the Job Methods instruction card before them.

- "**Check** to be sure that **each part of every step** has been considered."

- "Make **notes for constructive comments and questions** *after* demonstration is finished."

- "There will be **no discussion DURING demonstration—** only questions on points not clear."

Call on the first volunteer

- **Ask** the volunteer: "Is this **idea new?** Have you made a **present and** a **proposed breakdown?**"

- If either answer is **"NO"—call** on the **next volunteer**.

- **Have** the **volunteer follow** the **demonstration procedure** outlined above.

How to comment on each demonstration.

- **Compliment** the **volunteer on** the **good points** that show application of the Job Methods plan.

- Ask **members** if there are **questions about** the **demonstration** they want to ask or further improvements they want to suggest.

46

- **Discuss** the **application of each part of** the **4 steps** and exactly how they helped the supervisor make his improvement.

- **Stress:—"Was** it **worked out** with the **operator(s)?"—"How was credit given** (or planned)?"

- **Be sure you do not assume the attitude of an "expert." You should ONLY LEAD the discussion.**

- On **questions involving company policy,** the **supervisor** should be **referred to** the **management.**

- **Sum up** the **results of** the **improvements** in terms of increased production and machine use—savings in materials—better quality, safety, and housekeeping—etc. (use the blackboard)

- **Record each improvement on** the **Attendance Record and** on the **Proposal Report.**

Stress the use of STEP 3 during this practice period.

- **Show again** the **relation of STEP 2 to STEP 3.**

BLACKBOARD

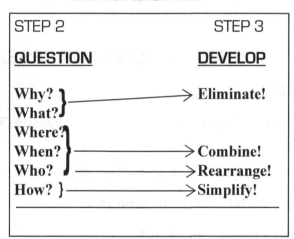

STEP 2	STEP 3
QUESTION	**DEVELOP**
Why? What?	→ Eliminate!
Where? When? Who?	→ Combine! → Rearrange!
How?	→ Simplify!

- **"Eliminating all unnecessary** details **eliminates waste.** This will **save manpower, machines,** and **materials** that are badly needed."

- **"Combining** and **rearranging** details **reduces handling and backtracking."**

- **"Simplifying** all **necessary details** by applying the principles on the card **makes** the **work easier** and **safer** for the operator."

- "Thus, we can produce **greater quantities** of **quality products** in **less time by** making the **best** possible **use of** the **manpower, machines, and materials available."**

(over)

Demonstrations No. 2, No. 3, No. 4 (same as No. 1).

- **"The four members who put on demonstrations** will write up their proposals and submit them at Session V."

*1 hr
45 min
to here*

- **"Those who put on their demonstrations at Session V will bring in their written proposals and revise them (if necessary) during the discussion periods."**

*Allow
10 min*

4. PROPOSALS ON SESSION III DEMONSTRATIONS

Ask members who put on demonstrations at Session III to read their written proposals to the group.

- Ask for **comments and suggestions.**

- **Recommend** that the **proposals, breakdown sheets,** sketches, samples, etc., **be submitted at once** for **approval and ACTION.**

- **Remind** the **group** it is important **to give credit** where credit is due.

- **Stress** the great importance of **continuing** to **search for better ways.**

*1 hr
55 min
to here*

- **Record** the **results of improvements on** the **Proposal Report.**

*Allow
5 min*

5. ASSIGN DEMONSTRATIONS FOR SESSION V
—AND CLOSE

Ask for remaining volunteers for Session V demonstrations.

- "Any **short job. Not** a **secret** product or process."

- **"Must be NEW improvements."**

- **"Follow** the **4-step plan."**

- "Make a **breakdown** of the **proposed** method."

- **Check** the **types of jobs** with volunteers.

- Invite **any who want help** to **stay** after Session.

Closing the session.

- Review the outstanding **improvements in** the **demonstration jobs and compliment** the **group on** their **progress.**

- Point out the **personal satisfaction and** the **advantages to** the **supervisor who increases production** by improving Job Methods.

- **Close promptly** with a reminder about Session V on

_____ from _____ to _____
  (Day)   (Hour)   (Hour)

- Collect **name cards**. Record attendance.

BEFORE YOU BEGIN SESSION V

BE SURE YOU HAVE THESE MATERIALS

Extra JM Instruction Cards   Extra Proposal Sheets
Extra Blank Breakdown Sheets   Proposal Reports
Attendance Record

BE AT PLANT 45 MINUTES BEFORE SESSION IS DUE TO OPEN

See the Plant Representative and review with him the PROPOSAL REPORT on the demonstrations made by members of the Group during Sessions II, III, and IV.

Tell the Plant Representative that in closing Session V you will ask each member of the Group to PLEDGE he will BREAKDOWN and QUESTION at least ONE JOB EVERY WEEK, and to PLEDGE he will DEVELOP and APPLY as many IMPROVEMENTS as possible on these jobs according to the Job Methods Plan.

In this discussion, strive to further develop the Plant Representative's interest so he will see that his Company's management gives constructive and continuing ENCOURAGEMENT to the Job Methods Plan and to the supervisors who have participated in it.

BE AT THE MEETING ROOM 15 MINUTES BEFORE SESSION IS DUE TO OPEN

Arrange chairs, look after ventilation, blackboard, crayon, erasers, etc.

REMEMBER

The emphasis in Session V is on STEP 4: Apply the new method.

WORK FROM THE OUTLINE—DON'T TRUST TO MEMORY

WITHIN TWO DAYS AFTER SESSION V

Make it a point to complete the ATTENDANCE RECORD and your PROPOSAL REPORT ON ALL DEMONSTRATIONS made by the group. Submit the ORIGINAL to the Plant Representative and one copy to the TWI DISTRICT OFFICE; keep a copy for yourself. See that the TWI DISTRICT OFFICE receives the Attendance Record PROMPTLY.

OUTLINE FOR SESSION V

1. OPENING THE SESSION

Opening remarks.

- Hand out **name cards**.

- **Express** your **appreciation of** the **interest** the Group has shown during the four sessions.

- **Compliment those who presented** constructive **improvements** at Session IV.

*5 min
to here*

- **Cite** one or two **recent improvements** which are **the result of applying the** Job Methods **Plan.**

2. REVIEW PREVIOUS SESSIONS

*Allow
5 min*

Review purpose and 4 steps of the Job Methods Plan.

- **Ask** the **group to give** the **4 steps and** state **purpose— without** looking at **instruction card.**

- **Review use of steps.**

BLACKBOARD

STEP 1 - **Breakdown** the Job
STEP 2 - **QUESTION** every Detail
STEP 3 - **DEVELOP** the New Method
STEP 4 - **APPLY** the New Method

*10 min
to here*

3. PRACTICE DEMONSTRATIONS—TWO JOBS

*Allow
1 hr
10 min*

Value of demonstrations.

- "Learn to **present new method before group**."

- "Develop **experience** by **observing how others improve** their Job **Methods**."

- "Through group discussion **we benefit** from the **experience of others**."

(over)

Ask each volunteer to follow this procedure.

- **Brief the following 8 points on the blackboard:**

See p. 75

1. "**Describe** briefly the **job** you have 'tackled' and explain samples and sketches you will use."

2. "Demonstrate the **present method.**"

3. "**Show present** method **breakdown and read details.**"

4. "Explain **what information** and leads you **obtained from** the **answers to the questions in STEP 2.**"

5. "Explain **how** this **information helped** you to **eliminate, combine, rearrange, and simplify** details **while developing** the **new method in STEP 3.**"

6. "Demonstrate the **proposed method.**"

7. "Explain **how you used**, or will use, the items under **STEP 4 to help** you **apply** the **new method.**"

8. "**Sum up** the **improvements** on your job."

Ask group members to follow the demonstration with the Job Methods instruction card before them.

- "**Check** to be sure that **each part of every step** has been considered."

- "Make **notes for comments and questions** to use **AFTER** demonstration is finished."

- "There will be **no discussion DURING demonstration**, only questions on points not clear."

Call on the first volunteer.

- **Ask** the volunteer: "Is this **idea new?** Have you made a **present and** a **proposed breakdown?**"

    If the answer to **either** is **"No," call** on the **next volunteer**.

- **Have** the **volunteer follow** the **demonstration procedure** outlined above.

How to comment on each demonstration.

- **Compliment** the **volunteer on** the **good points** that show application of the Job Methods plan.

- Ask **members** if there are **questions about** the **demonstration** they want to ask or further improvements they want to suggest.

- **Discuss** the **application of each part** of the **four steps** and exactly how they helped the supervisor make his improvement.

- **Stress:** "Was it **worked out** with the **operator(s)?**"—"**How was credit given** (or planned)?"

- **Be sure you do not assume the attitude of an "expert." You should ONLY LEAD the discussion.**

- On **questions involving company policy**, the **supervisor** should be **referred to** the **management**.

- **Sum up** the **results** of the **improvements** in terms of increased production and machine use, savings in materials, better quality, safety and housekeeping—etc. (use blackboard)

- **Record each improvement on** the **Attendance Record and** on the **Proposal Report**.

Stress the use of STEP 4 during this practice period.

- Discuss the **value of** a **complete, clear** and **concise write-up for** the "**Boss**."

    Also **breakdown sheets** (Present and Proposed), **sketches**, samples, **savings** in **manpower**, machines and materials.

- **Talk over** the various reasons why operators may need to be **sold** on the new method, even though it was **worked out** with one or more of them earlier (in Step 3).

- Discuss effective ways for **selling** new methods to operators.

- "Securing **final approval from all** concerned is **necessary to** assure **proper authorization** for making changes in methods **and to avoid difficulties**."

- Stress the **importance of quick action** in putting the new method to work.

    "Constant **checking** is **necessary to make sure** the new **method remains in effect**."

    "**Keep** on **searching for** a **better method**."

- "**Give** credit where credit is **due**."

    "**Credit is** a **powerful incentive** to producing more and better ideas."

    "**Credit** should be given to **every person who helped** make an improvement."

(over)

53

- "**Failure to give credit may stop all** other good **ideas** that might come from the Department or the Plant."

- "Proper **credit** is **indispensable to** the **success of** the Job Methods **plan**."

- **Ask the "Boss"** to give **credit** to **those who** have **helped** you.

Demonstration No. 2 (same as No. 1).

- **Sum up** the **improvements** on each job.

- **Record each improvement on Attendance Record** and on **Proposal Report**.

4. PROPOSALS ON SESSIONS IV AND V DEMONSTRATIONS

Ask members who put on demonstrations during sessions IV and V to read their completed proposals to the group.

- Ask for **comments** and **suggestions**.

- **Recommend** that the **proposals, breakdowns, etc.** be **submitted at once** for **approval and ACTION**.

- **Record results of improvements on** the **Proposal Report**.

5. REVIEW THE JOB INSTRUCTION PLAN

Stress the importance of instructing operators properly.

- "**Failure to properly instruct** operators **may mean failure** of the **new method**."

- "**To be sure** the **new method** is done **exactly right, instruct** the worker **carefully**—following the *Job Instruction Plan*."

Ask members to tell you the four get-ready points of the Job Instruction Plan.

1. "Have a **time table**."

2. "**Breakdown** the Job—**List** the **principal steps** and the **Key Points**."

3. "Have **everything ready**."

4. "Have the **work place** properly **arranged**."

Ask members to give the 4 basic steps of the Job Instruction plan (YOU review sub-heads briefly).

- "**Step 1—Prepare** the **worker**."

- "**Step 2—Present** the **operation**."

- "**Step 3—Try out performance**."

- "**Step 4—Follow up**."

- "'If the **worker hasn't learned**, the **instructor hasn't taught'** applies to **all jobs**."

*1 hr
50 min
to here*

- "**Be sure** this **plan** is **used every time** an **operator is instructed** in a New Method."

*Allow
10 min*

6. SUMMARY AND CLOSING APPEAL

Summarize the Job Methods Plan.

- **Review** the **purpose**.

   "**Carrying out** this **purpose** will **help** you **personally, and** it will **help win the war**."

- **Review** the **4 steps** completely.

   Be sure every member has an **instruction card**.

   Urge every member to **keep** the **instruction card** with him **and** to **use it every time** he begins **to improve** a Job **Method**.

   "All the **principles** that are **needed to improve hundreds** of our **jobs** are **on** this **card**."

The group member's responsibility.

- "Now that our five meetings are over and **each** of us has **demonstrated, 'it can be done,'** we have a **responsibility**. It **begins here and now**."

- "This **plan** is **only as good as we make it**—by applying it today, tomorrow, and every day to every job and keeping on applying it."

- **Ask** the **MEMBERS** of the group **TO PLEDGE** that they will **breakdown and question** at least **one job every week**.

   And to pledge they will **develop and apply** as many **improvements** on **these jobs** as they can.

- Assure the group of **management's support, and pledge to give** proposals **prompt action**.

(over)

Closing appeal.

- "Our **men and women** on the fighting front **are risking** their **lives to win this war** today, tomorrow, and every day of the week."

- "We all know by now that **improvements** in Job Methods **will** definitely **help** us p**roduce greater quantities of quality products in less time**."

- "I know you will **put** the **Job Methods plan to work** every time you can so you can do even more **for** the **war effort**."

- "And, I know that the **improvements** you make **will be** a **credit to you and** to the **company**."

- "Take time to **study every job. Encourage others** to take Job Methods so they can help."

- "It has been a **real pleasure to work with you**. I wish you the **best of success**."

- Record the attendance.

REFERENCE

MATERIAL

The following pages were prepared to assist you in your capacity as Trainer to make a convincing presentation. These pointers were prepared after hundreds of ten-hour sessions had been closely observed to find the best way to get results.

In presenting this Job Methods program, an otherwise convincing demonstration is often spoiled by a point that was improperly made because it appeared to be of minor importance. You will avoid this if you study the pages that follow. Practice the demonstrations until you have mastered each step and successfully timed your explanation with each move you make.

To help you become thoroughly competent in making the demonstrations, the explanations accompanying each step are given in full in this Reference Material. A clear understanding of the points to be made is absolutely necessary to a successful demonstration. These points are covered in detail on the pages which follow. References to these explanations appear in the Sessions Outline in the right hand margin and are printed in italics.

In addition, there are suggestions for establishing an informal atmosphere to put the group at ease; also, suggestions for making clear where the Job Methods program fits in as one of a supervisor's five needs.

Illustrations, stories, and examples of your own that show the practical application of the items presented are very desirable and should be used whenever appropriate. However, no item in the Sessions Outline is to be omitted or changed.

This does not mean that the paragraphs in quotation marks are always to be given to the group <u>exactly</u> word for word as given in the Sessions Outline. The Trainer may use his own words so long as the <u>exact meaning</u> is preserved at all times.

"ESTABLISH AN INFORMAL ATMOSPHERE"

The personal impression you make during the first 5 or 10 minutes is a big factor. If favorable, it makes the work easier. If unfavorable, you must make considerable effort later to overcome this impression.

The manner of your delivery and the tone of your voice should show clearly that you are in earnest, that you feel strongly about the importance of the work, and that you fully respect the present knowledge and experience of the group. Here are some ideas that will help you to open the session successfully.

1. Establish your own industrial background by briefly relating your own industrial connection. If this is done while writing or printing your name on the blackboard, it will set a pattern each one present will naturally follow.

- Have group members state their own connections briefly. This is done not so much for the information they give but to put them at ease. It is something they can do correctly and easily. Allow about 15 seconds for each member.

- Have members print their names and departments (and company's name, if several companies are represented) on a card which is placed before them.

- You can say that your difficulty in remembering names makes this cooperation on their part a help in conducting the sessions.

2. If plant regulations permit smoking, you may light a pipe or a cigarette and thus encourage informality. But keep in mind that a pipe or a cigarette can be a nuisance to you while trying to talk or write.

- When you have encouraged informality in this manner, put the pipe or cigarette aside until later in the session, when it will not interfere with conducting the meeting.

3. Your only purpose is to help them to make better use of what they now know. They were selected for their skill and experience. They probably know more about that part of their job than anyone else in their Department.

4. At all times avoid the atmosphere of the classroom. The members of your group are mature persons and they resent any suggestion of the "school teacher and school boy" relationship. Make it a point to avoid using terms such as "class," "student," "classroom," "teacher." Instead, use terms such as these: "group," "worker or learner," "get-together," "meeting," "instructor," etc. Keep before the group the fact that TRAINING is a normal part of a supervisor's job—it isn't something "special" or "apart." Think and speak of a meeting devoted to training just as you would of any other important meeting that has to do with PRODUCTION.

5. Tell the group they will discuss shop problems, as a group of men in the shop, and there's nothing technical.

- There will be a chance to actually try out the plan and practices discussed.

6. Tell the group that not so long ago you were "on their side of the table," when you took this training yourself. You know it is not too difficult to "get on to" and you have tried it out in practice. It works. Being able to "pass it along" is a satis-

faction to you. It's a real privilege to be associated with something that can be of so much help to the war effort.

THE FIVE NEEDS OF A SUPERVISOR

On the first page of the Outline for Session I, there is a paragraph which reads as follows: "Cover the **'five needs'** of **every supervisor.**" This appears near the middle of page 3. The Trainer's job at this point is to explain in a few words how Skill in Improving Job Methods is one of the supervisor's five most necessary qualifications.

Before you attempt to explain the five needs at this point, study the FIVE NEEDS STORY on page *ix*. Then, consider the following brief presentation given below as one way of telling this story clearly and in the shortest time.

Make it a point to take no more than three minutes at the outside to tell this story. Otherwise, your time table all through Session I will be upset.

Write the five needs on the blackboard as you tell the story.

"Let's look at a supervisor's job—and the knowledge and skill he must have to manage it successfully."

"First, he must have Knowledge of the Work." (Tell briefly what this covers and write on the blackboard: '1—Knowledge of Work'.)

"Second, he must have Knowledge of his Responsibilities." (Tell briefly what this covers and write on the blackboard: '2—Knowledge of Responsibilities'.)

"These two needs vary with each company and plant, and the necessary knowledge to fill these needs must be provided by the plant organization itself. Often knowledge that is necessary in one plant is of no use at all in another plant."

"A third need of every supervisor is Skill in Instructing." (Tell briefly what this covers and write on the blackboard: '3—Skill in Instructing'.)

"The fourth need is Skill in Improving Methods." (Tell briefly what this covers and write on the blackboard: '4—Skill in Improving Methods'.)

"And the fifth is Skill in Leading People." (Tell briefly what this covers and write on the blackboard: '5—Skill in Leading'.)

"The Skill in Improving Methods is the part of the supervisor's job that we're going to tackle in these Sessions. Training Within Industry gives the same kind of help on developing Skill in Instructing and Skill in Leading People."

"Practice and experience in using these three skills helps the supervisor to recognize and solve his daily problems. The supervisor who 'gets these three skills under his belt' can use them anywhere. They are his for all time."

THE DEMONSTRATION JOB

"The principles of the Job Methods plan can be best demonstrated by showing how they were applied to an actual job. The job we will use for demonstration is from another war plant—not this plant. Watch this demonstration job in terms of any job in your own department."

"While we have tried to pick a typical job as a sample for demonstration, it was impossible to select one that would be exactly like those performed in your shop or department. The sample job we picked out was chosen simply to show how the Plan definitely improves Job Methods."

"First we show you the PRESENT METHOD of doing this job, and then the PROPOSED METHOD. The same kinds of improvements that were made on this job can be made on any job which includes ONE or MORE of the three basic types of work."

JOB METHODS PLAN APPLIES TO ALL JOBS

Ask several members of the group to name the kinds of work done in their departments. From their answers, develop the fact that ALL of the operations on ANY production job can be classified under ONE or MORE of three basic types of work: (1) Material Handling (2) Machine Work (3) Hand Work.

(NOTE—Thinking, Inspection, and other "nonproductive" operations are parts of all three types of work)

Write the three types of work on the blackboard.

"The demonstration job includes: (1) Material Handling (2) Machine Work and (3) Hand Work. These are the features to be compared to your jobs—not this product, nor this operation. Make it a point to watch these three basic types of work during the demonstration; observe them in terms of any job in your own department."

Emphasize that these three types of work are included in the demonstration job and that these three types of work are comparable to their jobs. IT IS VERY NECESSARY TO MAKE THIS COMPARISON CLEAR. In this way you will overcome the objection that the Plan does not apply to their jobs because "their work is different." It reduces any job of any kind to the common denominator of ONE or MORE of the three general types of work.

MATERIAL AND EQUIPMENT

"The sample job selected for demonstration is the making and packing of Radio Shields. (SHOW SAMPLE RADIO SHIELD) Each Shield consists of a 5 inch by 8 inch Copper Sheet riveted to a similar Brass sheet, at four points. Each completed Shield has the word 'TOP' stamped in the lower right-hand corner of the Brass Sheet. The two sheets are each about fifteen one-thousandths, or one sixty-fourth of an inch thick (SHOW SAMPLE SHEETS). You will notice we are using cardboard in place of Copper and Brass because these metals are scarce and substitutes serve our purpose for the demonstration."

1. "The operations performed on the sheets are Inspecting, Assembling, Riveting, Stamping, and Packing."

2. "The operations are performed by FOUR OPERATORS, each working at his own bench."

3. "On each bench there is a hand-operated riveting machine represented by this paper stapler (SHOW THE STAPLER).

4. "The substitution will serve our purpose. It is impossible to carry riveting machines from group to group, and they are needed for war production."

5. "There is a rubber stamp and a stamp pad beside the riveting machine for the purpose of stamping each Shield" (SHOW THE STAMP AND PAD).

THE PRESENT METHOD

"We will now demonstrate the PRESENT METHOD of making and packing the Shields."

"There are four sets of machines and equipment, one for each of the four operators. We will follow the job of completing the Shields as performed by one of the operators whom we will call 'Jim Jones.' The same job was being done by the three other men. Another man, a Material Handler, worked with these operators. He serviced other operators on the same floor as well."

"The Copper and Brass sheets were delivered in Tote Boxes by the Material Handler at a point six feet away from the work bench. He brought the Shields from the Punching and Stamping Department. Two scrap bins, one for Copper and one for Brass, were located at the right of the bench. The Tote Box for Finished Shields was on the left side of the bench" (SHOW POSITIONS OF BOXES AND BINS).

Picking-up, Laying Out and Inspecting

"From his bench, Jones walked six feet to the Supply Box containing Copper Sheets. He picked up 15 to 20 Copper Sheets although he was only going to lay out 12 on the bench. He did not pick up the exact number of sheets because they were thin and it was hard to pick up the right number. Also, there were usually among them sheets that had been scratched or dented and they could not be used. With the Copper Sheets in one hand, he walked six feet back to the bench."

"Jones then laid out 12 sheets on the bench, in three rows of four to a row. As he laid them out, he inspected each one for scratches and dents. Only one side of the sheet had to be inspected because a scratch or dent bad enough to spoil its quality shows through. The sheets he rejected, he dropped into the Copper Scrap bin. To do this he had to take two steps toward the bin." (SHOW ONE OR TWO DAMAGED SHEETS AND PUT THEM IN THE BIN)

"Since a few sheets were usually left over, he walked back to the Supply Box and replaced the extra sheets. Then he walked three feet from the Copper Supply Box to the Brass Supply Box and picked up 15 to 20 Brass Sheets. Again, he did not pick up exactly 12 because the sheets were thin, and more than likely he would have had to scrap some of them."

"Jones then returned to the bench and inspected and laid out 12 Brass Sheets. He put one on top of each Copper Sheet. This had to be done carefully, since they scratched easily. Defective sheets were thrown in the Brass Scrap Bin. As before, he had to take two steps in order to throw the defective sheets into the proper bin (REJECT ONE OR TWO). If he had any Brass sheets left—usually he did—he had to make another trip to the Supply Box, six feet away, in order to return them and walk six feet back to the bench again."

"Jones then stacked the 12 sets of sheets crosswise (criss-cross) near the right side of the riveter and sat down in front of it."

Riveting and Completing the Shield

"He then picked up a set of sheets with his right hand, and lined them up so the holes matched and the edges of the sheets were even. The line-up tolerance was five one-thousandths of an inch. Lining up to this close tolerance called for a good deal of experience. When the sheets were lined up, he positioned them in the riveter, riveted the <u>top left</u>-hand corner, moved the sheets, riveted the other <u>top</u> corner, and removed them from the riveter. Then he reversed the sheets and riveted the bottom corners."

"He removed the Shield, reversed it, and placed it on the bench. He stamped the word `TOP' on the <u>right-hand</u> corner of the Brass Sheet, inking the stamp on the stamp pad. Then he set the completed Shield aside on the bench" (RIVET AND STAMP AT LEAST 3 SHIELDS).

"Having laid out 12 sets of sheets, he repeated the process described above until all 12 sets were riveted, stamped, and piled on the bench. Then he carried the 12 Shields to the Tote Box for Finished Shields, placed them in the box and returned to the bench."

Weighing and Packing

"He repeated this process until the Tote Box for Finished Shields was full. Then, he picked it up and carried it to the scale and weighed it. The scale, used by the entire department, was 50 feet away from his bench. The Tote Box weighed about 75 pounds, so a strong man was required. (PICK UP THE BASKET OR CHAIR YOU ARE USING AS A TOTE BOX AND CARRY IT TO THE REAR OF THE CONFERENCE ROOM. MAKE IT LOOK REALISTIC! USE PROPER LIFTING PROCEDURE.) Jones made out a weight ticket and placed it in the Tote Box. After placing the box beside the scale, he returned to his bench and started on another box of Shields."

"When two or three Tote Boxes of Finished Shields had accumulated near the scale, the Material Handler took them on a two-wheel hand truck to the Packing Department, a distance of 100 feet. In the Packing Department, the first thing the Packer did was to remove the Shields from the Tote Box, check-inspecting them as he went along. Then the Packer counted out 200 of them and packed them in a wooden case supplied by the Material Handler. The Packer nailed the cover on the case, weighed it, and stenciled the delivery address on the outside. He marked the weight on the delivery slip and set the case aside for shipment. The Tote Boxes he had emptied were returned by the Material Handler to a point close by the riveting operator's work bench."

<u>DISTRIBUTE PRESENT METHOD LAYOUT</u> and review the FLOW of MATERIAL from the supply boxes to the shipping platform. Point out the NUMEROUS HANDLINGS.

"Can you identify the Material Handling, the Machine Work, and the Hand Work that were performed on this job?" (REFER TO MATERIAL HANDLING, MACHINE WORK, AND HAND WORK ON THE BLACKBOARD AND HAVE VOLUNTEERS IN THE GROUP IDENTIFY EACH TYPE OF WORK.)

EQUIPMENT FOR THE PROPOSED METHOD

"Now, let's look at the PROPOSED METHOD for doing the same job. This improved method was developed with the help of the operator, Jim Jones, and put to work by the Foreman of the department by applying the principles of the Job Methods plan. For convenience, we will call the Foreman, Bill Brown."

"First, let's look at the improvement that was made. Then, we will discuss HOW Bill Brown applied this Job Methods plan and HOW each of us can use the Plan to improve any job in our department or company."

"Watch these improvements closely. Not only for the way in which they apply to this sample job but how the principles which made the improvements possible may be applied to ANY job in our department which includes Material Handling, Machine Work, or Hand Work."

"Here are the results: The Tote Boxes of Copper and Brass Sheets were placed directly on the bench by the Material Handler. It made no difference to him whether he placed them on the bench or six feet away. No extra work was required" (PLACE PILES OF SHEETS ON THE TABLE).

Riveting Machines, Fixtures and Jigs

"Two riveting machines were placed side by side on the bench. It was not necessary to buy new machines because the second machine was taken from one of the other benches. Then, a simple fixture was made to fit around the two riveters. The riveters were spaced very carefully—in exact locations so that rivets would go through two holes in the sheets at the same time. In addition, the fixture was equipped with two guides that fit the sheets. When the operator slips the sheets between the guides, the sheets are lined up automatically before riveting. This lining-up is within the tolerance limits of five one-thousandths of an inch." (SHOW GROUP HOW THE RIVETERS FIT INTO THE FIXTURE, AND HOW THE SHEETS FIT BETWEEN THE GUIDES, AND ARE AUTOMATICALLY LINED UP.)

"Two jigs were made to hold the sheets. (SHOW JIGS TO GROUP) One of them is for the Copper Sheets, the other for the Brass Sheets. One jig was placed at the right side of the fixture and the other at the left. An arm was placed on each jig at an angle of 45 degrees so the sheets are held in position where they can be easily picked up by the operator. This angle arm was suggested by Jim Jones."

"The Scrap Bins were placed under the work bench and two slots were cut in the bench so damaged sheets could be dropped into the bins. The slots are directly in front of the jigs. Cutting the slots was also suggested by Jim Jones, the operator."

New Arrangements for Packing and Shipping

"Shipping cases were placed beside the operator so he could put the completed shields directly into the shipping case. The Material Handler brings in empty cases and takes away the full ones."

"Since there were no longer any heavy Tote Boxes to be carried from one place to another and the sheets were lined up automatically, it became possible for operators with less experience and less physical strength to do the work satisfactorily. The result was that four strong, well-experienced operators were UPGRADED to more important work where this experience and these physical qualifications could be used to better advantage. Jim Jones was pleased that his contribution had helped improve the job."

THE PROPOSED METHOD

"Doing the job by the IMPROVED METHOD, the first thing the operator does is to put a pile of Copper Sheets in the right-hand jig and a pile of Brass Sheets in the left-hand jig."

"He 'fans' them out as he puts them into the jigs so they can be picked up one at a time very easily" (DEMONSTRATE BY FILLING THE JIGS).

"With his right hand, the operator picks up one Copper Sheet and with his left hand he picks up one Brass Sheet. He inspects both sheets, dropping any defective ones down the proper slot. And, he puts the good sheets together in pairs with the Brass Sheet on top. Then he puts each pair of sheets in the fixture. It is no longer necessary to line them up so the holes and edges will be in the same position. The guides on the fixture do this automatically."

The Simplified Riveting Process

"He rivets the <u>two bottom</u> corners <u>at the same time</u> since he has two riveting units and can operate them with two hands at the same time. Then he removes the sheets, reverses them, and places them in the fixture guides to rivet the <u>two top</u> corners. He does the bottom first, so the square corners will be flush against the guides on the fixture. Thus, he does not have to watch to see that the cut-away corners meet because, when the bottom has been riveted, the sheets are already very tightly pressed together and the cut-off corners meet exactly. As soon as it is riveted, he places the finished Shield in front of the fixture" (RIVET AT LEAST 3 SHIELDS).

"He repeats the process 19 more times until he has completed 20 Shields. He does not have to count or weigh them because the height of the fixture had been so designed that when 20 Shields are stacked in front of it, the top of the pile is exactly flush with the top surface of the fixture. The Shields are sold and delivered by count, not by weight."

"When he has finished 20 Shields, he places them in the shipping case at his right. As soon as one case has been filled with 200 Shields, he sets an empty case on the one he has just filled. When four or five cases are full, the Material Handler delivers the cases that are full to the Packing Department. There, the Shields are spot-check inspected by the Packer who nails on the cover, weighs the case, puts the weight on the delivery slip, and sets the case aside for shipment."

<u>DISTRIBUTE PROPOSED METHOD LAYOUT</u>. Point out the FLOW OF MATERIALS AND COMPARE WITH PRESENT METHOD LAYOUT.

"WHY THE TOP STAMP WAS UNNECESSARY"

"The stamp and stamp pad used in the PRESENT METHOD to put the word TOP on each completed Shield are not used under the PROPOSED METHOD. The reason is that Bill Brown, the Foreman, was in a position to ask the Engineering and Inspection Departments WHY this stamping was NECESSARY. He was given the following answer: 'Are you fellows still doing that? It is not necessary to stamp the word TOP on the newly designed Shields that have the upper left hand corner cut off. There is only one way they can be assembled NOW. The stamp should have been left off 6 or 8 months ago when the design was changed.'"

"Someone <u>forgot</u> to tell the Foreman about the stamp and <u>forgot</u> to change the blueprint and specifications."

HOW THE RIVETING DETAILS IN STEP 3 WERE SIMPLIFIED

Arrange the work place with the sheets ON the bench, packing case beside the operator, ONE riveting machine on the bench, and the CARD in YOUR HAND. Make a careful and logical explanation as you demonstrate ALL the significant moves and developments worked out by the foreman.

"Let's see how Bill Brown, with some help from his operator, Jim Jones, simplified the details noted 'better way.' He used these principles and ONLY these principles."

This is the way Bill said he reasoned out the improvements. He used the card to get ideas.

- He read: "PRE-POSITION the materials in the proper work area."

    - He moved the sheets near the riveting machine.

    - But they were still awkward to pick up.

- Again he consulted the card: "Use JIGS and fixtures for holding."

This gave him an idea. Why not make jigs to hold the sheets?

    - Jim Jones suggested putting an angle arm that would fan out the sheets on each jig, so he could always pick up one sheet with each hand.

    - So Bill had the jigs made up.

    - But it was still necessary to LINE UP the sheets by hand.

    - Also one hand had to be used for holding while doing the riveting.

    - As Bill studied the problem an idea developed: Since there were two punchings, why not try TWO riveting machines?

- He looked at the card and read: "Use jigs and FIXTURES for holding."

    - This seemed to be a good idea, so he had a fixture designed to HOLD and EXACTLY SPACE the riveting machines.

    - Once the fixture was made, he saw at a glance the need for guides to line up the sheets.

    - Now, one hand need not be used for holding. BOTH HANDS could be used for riveting.

As Bill and Jim tried out the improvement, they came to a defective sheet. It was necessary to get up and go to the scrap bin to get rid of it.

- They consulted the card again: "Use drop delivery chutes."

    - The operator picked up this idea and asked whether slots could not be cut in the bench.

    - This was done and the scrap boxes were placed under the slots.

- Now, it was NOT necessary to get up so as to discard scrap.

- Bill then made the job still "EASIER" by having the fixture made of just the right thickness so that a pile of 20 completed Shields would be flush with the top of the fixture.

   - The empty cases for finished Shields WERE PRE-POSI-TIONED within easy reach.

   - Then it was a simple matter to place the Shields directly in the packing cases until they were filled.

"This was the REASONING Bill went through, with some help from one of his workmen, when they worked out the proposed method. They used the principles on the card and only these principles.

THE 8 STEPS OF A PRACTICE DEMONSTRATION

A great help to the Trainer and the group members is to list on the blackboard (in very abbreviated form) the 8 steps for putting on a practice demonstration. These demonstrations take place during Sessions II, III, IV and V.

In their briefest form, without regard to conventional abbreviation, the 8 points would be written like this:

1. Describe the job

2. Demo present method

3. Read details—present

4. Info. from Step 2

5. How info. used in Step 3

6. Demo proposed method

7. How use Step 4

8. Sum up

HOW TO IMPROVE
JOB METHODS

A practical plan to help you produce GREATER QUANTITIES of QUALITY PRODUCTS in LESS TIME, by making the best use of the **Manpower, Machines, and Materials now available.**

STEP I — BREAK DOWN the job.
1. List **all** details of the job **exactly** as done by the **Present Method**.
2. Be sure details include all:
   - Material Handling.
   - Machine Work.
   - Hand Work.

STEP II — QUESTION every detail.
1. Use these types of questions:
   WHY is it necessary?
   WHAT is its purpose?
   WHERE should it be done?
   WHO is best qualified to do it?
   HOW is the "best way" to do it?

2. Also question the:
   Materials, Machines, Equipment, Tools, Product Design, Layout, Work-place, Safety, Housekeeping.

STEP III — DEVELOP the new method.
1. ELIMINATE **unnecessary** details.
2. COMBINE details when practical.
3. REARRANGE for better sequence.
4. SIMPLIFY all **necessary** details:
    - Make the work **easier** and **safer.**
    - **Pre-position** materials, tools, and equipment at the best places in the **proper work area.**
    - Use **gravity-feed** hoppers and **drop-delivery** chutes.
    - Let **both hands** do **useful** work.
    - Use **Jigs** and **Fixtures** instead of hands, for holding work.
5. **Work out** your idea **with** others.
6. Write up your proposed new method.

STEP IV—APPLY the new method.
1. **Sell** your proposal to the **boss.**
2. **Sell** the new method to the **operators.**
3. Get final approval of all concerned on **Safety, Quality, Quantity, Cost.**
4. Put the new method to work. Use it until a **better** way is developed.
5. Give **credit** where credit is due.

———————

Job Methods Training Program
OFFICE OF PRODUCTION MANAGEMENT
War Manpower Commision

Publications from Enna

From Enna's new classics by Shigeo Shingo to our books and training packages regarding operational excellence, Enna provides companies with the foundation of knowledge and practical implementation ideas that will ensure your efforts to internalize process improvement. Reach your vision and mission with the expertise within these world-class texts. Call toll-free (866) 249-7348, visit us on the web at www.enna.com to order, or request our free product catalog.

Enjoy the rest of the books in our T.W.I. Training Series:

Job Instruction: Sessions Outline and Materials

Job Instruction, a short, intensive training program, was developed in order to provide skills in leadership to new and experienced supervisors alike. Contained within the Job Instruction book are samples, scenarios, and discussion topics which give you the tools necessary to properly instruct new workers and do away with waste and accidents, as well as cut down the time it takes to get a new worker 'up to speed' on his job.
ISBN 978-1-897363-92-8 | 2009 | $34.99 | Item: **922**

Job Methods: Sessions Outline and Materials

In teaching you the method behind the job and how to properly break down a job into its most fundamental parts, this book aims to teach you how to reduce wasteful behavior and wasteful steps within a job. The training material within provides you with worksheets, forms and sample scenarios to give you practice in scrutinizing and simplifying jobs.
ISBN 978-1-897363-93-5 | 2009 | $34.99 | Item: **923**

Job Relations: Sessions Outline and Materials

Job Relations was developed in order to provide management with a tool whereby supervisors could acquire skills in leadership. Contained within the Job Relations book are sample scenarios, discussion topics and instructional diagrams that relate the supervisor and his subordinates, show the dynamic of such a relationship and provide a way of looking at and dealing with these relationships that will benefit everyone in the company.
ISBN 978-1-897363-94-2 | 2009 | $34.99 | Item: **924**

Union Job Relations: Sessions Outline and Materials

Union Job Relations was developed concurrently with Job Relations in order to provide stewards with a way to acquire skills in leadership within their company and union. Contained within the Union Job Relations book are sample scenarios, discussion topics and instructional diagrams that relate the steward to his union, supervisors and the union members he is responsible for, shows the dynamic of such relationships and provide a way of looking at and dealing with these relationships that will benefit everyone in the company.
ISBN 978-1-897363-95-9 | 2009 | $34.99 | Item: **925**

To Order: Enna Corp., 1602 Carolina Street, Unit B3, Bellingham, WA 98229

Program Development Institute

The Program Development Institute was established in order to train people in setting up and implementing an entire training program within their company. Enclosed are worksheets, examples and practice problems to assist in developing the program as a training coordinator. With this book you will learn how to step back and look at the company as a whole, before implementing training and improvements.
ISBN 978-1-897363-96-6 | 2009 | $34.99 | Item: **926**

Problem Solving Training: Sessions Outline and Materials

The Problem Solving workbook instructs on how to properly Isolate, Breakdown, Question and Solve problems. From detailing just how you know you have a problem to charts and diagrams that will assist you in solving the problem, this book is a must read for anyone who deals with production on a daily basis.
ISBN 978-1-926537-00-9 | 2009 | $34.99 | Item: **927**

Bulletin Series

Based on the simple premise that in order to function there has to be an organized structure that recognizes that ongoing training is an investment that will always pay for itself the T.W.I. Bulletin Series is packed with ideas, concepts, and methods that will produce results. Contained within are bulletins that will assist in selecting supervisors, strengthening management and achieving continuous results.
ISBN 978-1-897363-91-1 | 2008 | $34.99 | Item: **914**

Other Books by Enna

Mistaken Kanbans

Let Mistaken Kanbans be your roadmap to guide you through the steps necessary to implement and successful Kanban System. This book will help you to not only understand the complexities of a Kanban System but gives you the tools necessary, and the guidance through real-life lessons learned, to avoid disastrous consequences related to the improper use of such systems.
ISBN 978-1-926537-10-8 | 2009 | $27.99 | Item: **919**

The Toyota Mindset

From the brilliant mind of a legend in the LEAN manufacturing world comes the reasoning behind the importance of using your intellect, challenging your workers and why continuous improvement is so important. For anyone who wishes to gain insight into how the Toyota Production System came to be or wants to know more about the person behind TPS this book is a must read!
ISBN 978-1-926537-11-5 | 2009 | $34.99 | Item: **920**

Phone: 1+ (360) 306-5369   **Fax:** (905) 481-0756   **Email:** info@enna.com

The Toyota Way in Sales and Marketing

Many companies today are trying to implement the ideas and principles of Lean into non-traditional environments, such as service centers, sales organizations and transactional environments. In this book Mr. Ishizaka provides insight on how to apply Lean operational principles and Kaizen to these dynamic and complicated environments.
ISBN 978-1-926537-08-5 | 2009 | $28.99 | Item: **918**

Training Packages

5S Training Package

Our 5S Solution Packages will help your company create a sustainable 5S program that will turn your shop floor around and put you ahead of the competition. All of the benefits that come from Lean Manufacturing are built upon a strong foundation of 5S. Enna's solution packages will show you how to implement and sustain an environment of continuous improvement.
Version 1: Sort, Straighten, Sweep, Standardize and Sustain
ISBN 978-0-973750-90-4 | 2005 | $429.99 | Item: **12**
Version 2: Sort, Set In Order, Shine, Standardize and Sustain
ISBN 978-1-897363-25-6 | 2006 | $429.99 | Item: **17**

Study Mission to Japan

We are excited to present an exclusive trip to the birthplace of Lean. We provide a one-week unique tour at a reasonable all-inclusive price that will guide you to a better understanding of Lean Manufacturing principles. Enna has exclusive access to Toyota and Toyota suppliers due to our publications of Dr. Shigeo Shingo's classic manuscripts. You will have one-on-one access to Japanese Lean Executives and learn from their experiences and solutions. We also offer custom private tours for executive management teams over 12 people. Join us on our next tour by visiting www.enna.com/japantrip and register on-line or by telephone at: +1 (360) 306-5369

To Order:

Mail orders and checks to:
Enna Products Corporation
ATTN: Order Processing
1602 Carolina Street, Unit B3
Bellingham, WA 98229, USA
Phone: +1 (360) 306-5369 • Fax: (905) 481-0756
Email: info@enna.com

We accept checks and all major credit cards.
Notice: All prices are in US Dollars and are subject to change without notice.

To Order: Enna Corp., 1602 Carolina Street, Unit B3, Bellingham, WA 98229